MW00423616

Stunning

by David Adjmi

A SAMUEL FRENCH ACTING EDITION

FOUNDED 1830

NEW YORK HOLLYWOOD LONDON TORONTO

SAMUELFRENCH.COM

ISBN 978-0-573-69781-4   Printed in U.S.A.   #29209

MUSIC USE NOTE

Licensees are solely responsible for obtaining formal written permission from copyright owners to use copyrighted music in the performance of this play and are strongly cautioned to do so. If no such permission is obtained by the licensee, then the licensee must use only original music that the licensee owns and controls. Licensees are solely responsible and liable for all music clearances and shall indemnify the copyright owners of the play and their licensing agent, Samuel French, Inc., against any costs, expenses, losses and liabilities arising from the use of music by licensees.

IMPORTANT BILLING AND CREDIT
REQUIREMENTS

All producers of *STUNNING* *must* give credit to the Author of the Play in all programs distributed in connection with performances of the Play, and in all instances in which the title of the Play appears for the purposes of advertising, publicizing or otherwise exploiting the Play and/or a production. The name of the Author *must* appear on a separate line on which no other name appears, immediately following the title and *must* appear in size of type not less than fifty percent of the size of the title type.

In addition the following credit *must* be given in all programs and publicity information distributed in association with this piece:

Originally produced in March 2008 by
Woolly Mammoth Theatre Company, Washington DC,
Howard Shalwitz, Artistic Director; Jeffrey Hermann, Managing Director

Produced by Lincoln Center Theatre, New York City, 2009

STUNNING was first produced by the Woolly Mammoth Theater Company in Washington D.C. on March 1, 2008. The performance was directed by Anne Kauffman, with sets by Dan Conway, costumes by Helen Huang, lighting by Colin K. Bills, sound by Ryan Rumery, dialect coaching by Sasha Olinick, and fight choreography by John Gurski. The cast was as follows:

BLANCHE	Quincy Tyler Bernstine
JOJO	Clinton Brandhagen
IKE	Michael Gabriel Goodfriend
SHELLY	Gabriels Fernandez-Coffey
LILY	Laura Heisler
CLAUDINE	Abby Wood

CHARACTERS

LILY SCHWECKY – *(sixteen)* Truly "cute", slight, naifish, something of an oddball. The "baby" – she's sixteen going on about 11; she's a bit regressed. Her mind works quickly but her thoughts are incredibly scattered. A follower, but it's more out of a need for connectedness than an innate passivity.

BLANCHE NESBITT – *(forties)* Lily's new housekeeper, African American, an extremely intelligent, voluble, and terribly sensitive autodidact. Damaged, but maintains a great sense of irony and dry humor. She adapts to survive – she's performative, and the performance wears her down eventually. An outsider.

IKEY SCHWECKY – *(forty-five)* Lily's new husband: controlling, brute, bumptious, but there's something fragile in him, broken – he's more transparent than he thinks.

SHELLY – *(early-twenties)* Lily's big sister; a leader; she's got a stentorian quality, but naturalizes this by cultivating "girly" preoccupations. The laziness of her r's and a's feels calculated and somehow hostile.

JOJO – *(thirties, early forties)* Shelly's uxorious husband; basically a good guy but limited; rather put upon, has trouble sticking to his guns.

CLAUDINE – *(nineteen)* a bit hysterical; unselfconscious – even brute – in her bids for approval. She has a desperate conformity.

SETTING

The play takes place largely within the confines of the midwood section of Brooklyn – a very affluent, largely Jewish area; one which exerts a centripetal force on the people who live there. Despite the proximity to Manhattan, there's a provincialism to it, an insularity, but also an extremely tight-knit sense of community.

TIME

Around now.

A NOTE ON STYLE

The play shifts styles.

While it is concerned with psychological reality it only intermittently correlates with the detail or psychological consistency usually associated with Realism. There are deliberate and drastic alternations in tone, style, etc., that happen scene by scene, within scenes and between beats with no transition. It is therefore critical for actors to follow the rhythms of the play, as it is scored; the psychological truth can be extracted from this.

It is crucial that the shifts and transitions in the piece, no matter how abrupt, are rooted in an emotional reality.

NOTE ON TEXT

Sometimes I think of my plays as cubist, because they juxtapose elements that don't seem to go together – genres, styles, emotions, tonalities. There is a liquidity to them, a deliberate and precisely honed instability. The plays go wrong in production when things are smoothed out and normalized. The worlds of these plays are fractured, and the notational system (which can be maddening to read on the page, I admit it) is a way to delineate how they're fractured.

A double slash (//) indicates either an overlap or a jump – i.e., no break between the end of one character's speech and the beginning of the following speech.

Speech in parentheses indicates either a sidetracked thought within a conversation, or a shift in tone or emphasis with no temporal break, no pause or beat or transition.

A STOP, DISAMBIGUATED

A STOP is a pause followed by either a marked shift in tone or tempo (like a cinematic jumpcut or a quantum leap) or no change in tempo whatsoever – somewhat like putting a movie on pause and then pressing play.

STOPs aren't empty or merely ambient, they are "full" – i.e., the tension needs to first build – or drop – invisibly inside of them (again, the quantum analogy is a good one) and then explode – or dissipate – seemingly "out of nowhere." Because STOPs are all about tension they should be marked by physical stillness.

STOPs happen with NO psychological transition – the energy needs to either build or dissipate inside the pause. These moments are, in a way, the key to playing my work. If you can figure out the STOPs you can eventually figure out the play.

SET

I know three things about the set for this play: 1. Continuing the homage to Douglas Sirk and Tennessee Williams (And Plato too, from *The Republic*) mirrors are very important to this world. It would not be out of keeping with the tenor of the play (and the themes of illusion, imitation, deception, whatever) to selectively stage whole scenes, parts of scenes, sections of the stage using full length mirrors (think "las meninas" or even "the lady from shanghai") keeping in mind, obviously, that this can't be used egregiously; 2. The world of the play is bleached out, whitewashed – there's no color in it save for various shades of white, and transparent surfaces, glass, mirrors, etc.; 3. The set should have some kind of motility: it isn't stable; it wants to move, it wants to transform, whether with panels, walls, rollers, I'm not sure but perspectives can shift.

–David Adjmi

GLOSSARY OF SYRIAN-AMERICAN TERMS

ABOOSE – "Oh, how sweet and adorable."

CA-AN – (ca as in "cat" and an as in "ann") Spoken when challenging the veracity of something. Has a vaguely sarcastic connotation, as in "yeah, right!" – sometimes serves as phatic punctuation.

DIBEH – Slang for idiot (female), DIB (male).

ERT – An exclamation of disgust or revulsion.

HEEE – Not a word but a sharp intake of breath indicating shock, concern, surprise or worry.

GAZZY – Silly and fun.

GAZZCASE (with a hard A, as in "Lair") – Playful term for a someone who is mentally disorganized, a kind of screwball.

IBE (with a hard A, silent E) – Comment on "shameful" or inappropriate behavior.

OBDEH – (ob as in "obverse") Person of african descent (f), *OBID* (m).

OOLIE – An exclamation of shock, worry, horror, discovery – and spoken with correlative intonations (reverential worry: "ooooolllllliiieeeee," "OO!LIE!", OOLIE!, etc).

SHOOF, SHOOFIE – (A command) "look!": as in "shoof haddie" ("look at her").

SKETCHING – Slang for kidding or joking.

TRANSLATION FROM SPANISH

SPANISH: *Ella me decia: "Lily tú eres un angel, y tu pelo es de ceda te quiero como mi hija"*
ENGLISH: She told me: "Lily you are an angel, and your hair is silk I love you like a daughter

SPANISH: *Yo tambien te puedo mecer en el columpio vamos al parque ahora mismo!!*
ENGLISH: I could push you on the swing too!! Let's go to the park right now!!

SPANISH: *Todavía estamos trabajando Anna maria la luz está a tu derecha.*
ENGLISH: We're still working Anna maria the light is on your right.

SPANISH: *Ojalá no se enoje.*
ENGLISH: I hope he doesn't get mad.

SPANISH: *El no se enterará.*
ENGLISH: He won't find out.

SPANISH: *¿Me lastimó, viste lo que hizo?*
ENGLISH: He hurt me did you see what he did?

SPANISH: *Tengo que irme de aquí; promete que nos iremos.*
ENGLISH: I have to get out of here – promise we'll leave.

SPANISH: *Y a tí que te importa nos vamos para Chicago.*
ENGLISH: What do you care? We're going to Chicago.

SPANISH: *Mira hacia atrás, no me conviertas en piedra.*
ENGLISH: Look back, don't turn me to stone.

SPECIAL THANKS

(in no order)

Rebecca Taichman, Lisa Portes, Morgan Jenness, Mark Subias, Adam Greenfield, Polly Carl, Stephen Willems, New York Theatre Workshop, Paige Evans, Andre Bishop, Emily Shooltz, Dartmouth College, Danny Mastrgiorgio, Quincy Tyler Bernstine, Laura Heisler, Charlayne Woodard, Cristin Milioti, Michael Goodfriend, Gabrielle Fernandez-Coffey, Abby Wood, Clint Brandhagen, Lecy Gorenson, Jeneane Serralles, Sas Gioldberg, Steve Rattazzi, Nilaja Sun, April Yvette Thompson, Howard Shalwitz, Elissa Goetschius, Miriam Weisfeld, Woolly Mammoth Theatre, Paul Rusconi, Heidi Schreck, Kip Fagan, Jim McCarthy and Gloria Peterson, Anne Kaufman, Tory Stewart, Kath Tolan, Philip Himberg and all my friends at Sundance, Olivier Sultan, Corinne Hayoun. And to all the actors who participated in countless readings, workshops, etc. of this play who weren't mentioned here. Thank you.

ACT ONE

The Ambassadors

1.

*(**CLAUDINE**'s house.)*

(A card game.)

*(Three girls sitting at a card table: **SHELLY**, **LILY**, **CLAUDINE**.)*

(They all have nearly identical feathered hair modeled after the 70's "Farrah" look from Charlie's Angels. They all have bangles – meretriciously loud bangles – on their wrists; this is an index of wealth.)

(They all have variations of the same boots, clothes – one gets the sense that no one does anything in this world without the tacit agreement of the others.)

*(**LILY** is painfully, comically sunburnt and peeling for most of this act.)*

(The play opens with a virtuosic shuffling of the cards.)

(rapid fire:)

SHELLY. Stick to the rules //

LILY. Where's // Tuni?

SHELLY. Jacks or better nothing wild everybody // in?

LILY. We have to wait for Tuni but-h.

CLAUDINE. Tuni's not coming she's getting a divorce.

SHELLY. She's //

CLAUDINE. Ye you didn't // hear she's

SHELLY. Whaddayou*sketching?* //

CLAUDINE. separating from (no-I'm-not-sketching) she's separated // from

11

LILY. Oolie! //

SHELLY. She just got married!

LILY. She had a baby //

CLAUDINE. YE and the baby I think it has like a down's *syn-drome?*

SHELLY. HEEE //

CLAUDINE. (Aduknow) //

LILY. And she //

CLAUDINE. (or like) //

SHELLY. I //

CLAUDINE. *and they hid it* //

SHELLY. *(to LILY)* (Stop-playing-with-your-hands) //

CLAUDINE. and Tuni had to take it in to see a *specialist* //

LILY. Wheh?

CLAUDINE. in the *ity-cay* This *y-gay* //

SHELLY. (You're-making-me-nervous-stop-it) //

CLAUDINE. (I think it was Mount Sinai) //

SHELLY. *(fixes earring)* (I-had-my-transplant-theh) //

CLAUDINE. And like the husband // like

> **(SHELLY** *pulls a packet of juicy fruit, puts down the cards.)*

LILY. Did she have a // girl?

CLAUDINE. he like //

LILY. *(imagining a cute baby:)* Aboose.

SHELLY. *(to CLAUDINE)* (You want?)

CLAUDINE. And then I (no-it's-not-sugahless) and I think he was rejecting the kid // or

> **(LILY** *accepts a stick of gum, chews.)*

SHELLY. I thought //

CLAUDINE. or no, YEAH // and he

LILY. Heeee //

CLAUDINE. goes "I don't want *you?* and I don't want this *kid?* and // gimme a divorce"

LILY. With the *down's* syndrome // *kid?!*

SHELLY. Dib Who's the husband.

CLAUDINE. Morris Betesh //

SHELLY. Piece a shit.

CLAUDINE. No-Ye-He-is-a-piece-//-a-shit

LILY. Who's he related to?

CLAUDINE. Schweckies of Avenue P.

SHELLY. That's not a good // family

CLAUDINE. *(munching violently on a carrot stick) Piece a shit* //

LILY. Do they own Duane Reade? //

SHELLY. THAT'S YA SECOND COUSIN DUANE READE //

CLAUDINE. *(vicious) They have a bad* // *reputation*

LILY. What do they own //

CLAUDINE. *(finger wagging tone)* Bad family //

SHELLY. And I go to her I go //

CLAUDINE. *(vicious)* BAD //

SHELLY. I go don't marry this jerk //

CLAUDINE. Me too!

SHELLY. (And-remembah?!-and-I-go) //

CLAUDINE. Me-*too*-everyone-her-mother-*Debby* //

SHELLY. and now she's // screwed

CLAUDINE. And-I-//-go.

SHELLY. fogettaboutit //

CLAUDINE. *(shaking her hand as if it's burned)* Yeah-*oh-figget-*//-*it*

SHELLY. *(mimicking her hand shaking) Ooooolie figetiiiiiiit* //

CLAUDINE. (She // screwed herself)

SHELLY. She's // finished

CLAUDINE. She committed // suicide

LILY. (Oolie!) //

CLAUDINE. RUINED!!

   [STOP]

CLAUDINE. *(crunching a carrot stick)* I like the dip What's in this //

LILY. Chives

CLAUDINE. *(bright)* Heeee. I *like* chives //

LILY. Should we // play?

CLAUDINE. *(quick)* (Did you see Debbie's haih? She cut // it)

SHELLY. I like your bangles //

LILY. *(exhibiting her wrist)* Sheri-got-me-for-my-showah

CLAUDINE. *(muffled resentment)* Your wrist looks thin.

LILY. I gained weight-h //

SHELLY. Ca-an she's a *stick!*

CLAUDINE. *(a little too loud)* You're BLACK!

SHELLY. She's a Obdeh. //

LILY. From the panama jack.

CLAUDINE. *Obdeh*

SHELLY. She always // gets black

CLAUDINE. *(singsong)* HOW WAS ARUBA-AAAAA?

LILY. Stunning.

SHELLY. *(singsong)* Ye-eee-eeeee?

CLAUDINE. Dibeh-you-nevah-said-nothing-You-got-back-when.

LILY. Yestiday //

CLAUDINE. (Ack-blay) //

SHELLY. You flew Delta? //

LILY. United.

SHELLY. WITH THE TERRORISTS – ah?!

CLAUDINE. LEAVE HAH.

SHELLY. Whatditellyou.

LILY. Ikey bought the // tickets, I

CLAUDINE. You look STUNNING.

SHELLY. *(chews gum efficiently)* (Mommy wants you // to cawl hah)

CLAUDINE. You look UNNING-STAY.

SHELLY. cawl hah // cell

LILY. *(juts out her arm)* I'm peeling. shoof

CLAUDINE. Was the sand pink. //

LILY. *(peels an enormous swatch of skin)* SHOOFIE.

CLAUDINE. HEEEE. Put // cream!

SHELLY. *(mean)* Dibeh ya hafta put cream!

LILY. I put-h!!

CLAUDINE. Is the house finished Wheh's Ikey?

LILY. We just moved in //

CLAUDINE. Did you go jetskiing? //

LILY. The water was choppy //

CLAUDINE. But-it's-fun-right-isn't-it-I-TOLD-YOU-right //

LILY. I //

CLAUDINE. Isn't it I know.

   [STOP]

SHELLY. You're *egnant-pray?*

LILY. *(wide-eyed)* Aduknow.

SHELLY. Ca-an.

LILY. He wants to start // soon.

CLAUDINE. Is the house finished //

SHELLY. Excited?

LILY. Ye.

CLAUDINE. I want kids.

SHELLY. You'll have-h!

CLAUDINE. I'm sick of living with my mothah.

SHELLY. I told you I would set you up

CLAUDINE. with *Stevie* //

LILY. *(revulsion)* Ert //

CLAUDINE. THIS IS HOW HE DANCES //

SHELLY. He comes from a good // family.

CLAUDINE. *(practically hyperventilating)* I'm nineteen-h! //

LILY. *(gingerly)* Ya bracelet is shahp

CLAUDINE. (My-cousin-makes-bracelets-she-sells-them-at-flea-markets.)

SHELLY. *(blame)* You don't go to parties //

CLAUDINE. YOU SOUND LIKE *MY MOTHAH.*

SHELLY. Do guys like whiney girls NO.

CLAUDINE. *(covers her face, emotionally exhausted)* I'm old.

LILY. (I feel old.)

CLAUDINE. Bonnie has four kids //

SHELLY. (Three) //

CLAUDINE. and she's two years younger than me I'm gonna be twenny.

LILY. If I met someone you will.

CLAUDINE. But you're pretty.

LILY. You're stunning!

CLAUDINE. I'M FAT!

LILY. Look at my // calves

CLAUDINE. *(looking in a mirrored surface)* No-I-have-//-crows-feet

SHELLY. *(reapplying lipstick)* I like your // oots-bay

LILY. I'm // fat

CLAUDINE. (I got those at loehmann's) //

LILY. I feel old.

CLAUDINE. SHUT UP YA FREAKIN TWELVE-ah.

LILY. I'm seventeen next week.

　　　[STOP]

CLAUDINE. I feel more secure in myself; don't you think I'm more secure in myself than I was this time last-chyee //

LILY. I like your bracelet //

CLAUDINE. (*Errrrrt*, I *hate* this bracelet, it's disgusting.)

SHELLY. How's the house?

LILY. Big.

CLAUDINE. I heard it's stunning

　　　(beat)

LILY. There's a ghost.

SHELLY. Whadayou *tawking* about?

LILY. Ikey said there was, and then I saw it the other night.

(short pause)

SHELLY. There's no ghost.

(pause)

LILY. I saw it. *(beat; then to **SHELLY**)* I miss Mommy and Daddy.

SHELLY. Don't be such a freakin baby.

(beat)

*(**LILY**, somewhat abstracted, lifts her thumb to her mouth, grazing the tip of her lip; **SHELLY** sees this – pushes it back down in her lap.)*

LILY. *(regaining awareness)* It's weird. Aduknow.

[STOP]

CLAUDINE. I saw Stevie on the holiday I saw Stevie I saw Ralphie // I saw

SHELLY. Are we gonna play or what.

CLAUDINE. Three card draw.

LILY. Deal //

SHELLY. (Five.)

CLAUDINE. *(to **LILY**, regarding some pastry)* Pass that //

(Loud music cuts her off.)

2.

(**LILY** *and* **BLANCHE**)

(An interview)

(**LILY** *and* **IKE**'s *home in Midwood, Brooklyn*)

(The house is all white – perhaps several shades of white, but white. There is no color in this set. The minimalism **LILY** *espouses is that of the arid, philistine, nouveau riche – no art or anything – but terribly impressive in its own bombastic right.)*

(A vase of dilapidated chrysanthemums in a vase on a mantel. Lots of reflective surfaces.)

(A fishbowl with a lonely confused little goldfish swimming in circles – a single charged node of color in an otherwise colorless room.)

(**LILY**'s *outfit has an element of a girl playing dress-up – which thwarts the attempt at sophistication. She has a checklist in hand.* **BLANCHE** *stands out like a sore thumb.)*

LILY. What's your name?

BLANCHE. Blanche.

LILY. *(quizzical)* Isn't that something you do to vegetables?

BLANCHE. I don't cook. //

LILY. *(mild suspicion)* Do you do windows?

BLANCHE. (Yeah and I iron) //

LILY. *(vague panic)* Tennis skirts?

BLANCHE. *(desperate retraction) But I could learn to //* cook

LILY. (Because-they're-white-and-if-you-burn-them-I'll-freak).

BLANCHE. I won't.

    (beat)

LILY. Are you detail-oriented?

BLANCHE. Uh-huh.

LILY. Like "orientated towards the details"?

BLANCHE. *(nonplussed)* (Isn't that what that // means?)

LILY. I play tennis Wednesdays and Fridays //

BLANCHE. *(chummy)* Oh I used to play *squash* //

LILY. *(unbroken sentence)* it's good for this *(points to arm)* feel this *(gestures)* it's a great spoht tennis.

BLANCHE. *(feeling and talking at the same time)* But that was a long time ago.

LILY. *(points to hip)* It's good for this.

BLANCHE. (Supple) //

LILY. But my backhand is suffering //

BLANCHE. *Pity* //

LILY. And you have to use bleach! I'm very meticulous about everything and I have ways I like things done; I like things a certain way, I'm meticulous. *(aimlessly sprinkles fish food)* "Hiiiiiiiiieeee" *(to* **BLANCHE***; still sprinkling)* that's Kitty // it gets fed once

BLANCHE. *(looks for a cat)* Where?

LILY. in the morning – "hiiiiii" (But-don't-overfeed-it-cuz-you'll-kill-it.)

BLANCHE. The *fish?*

LILY. Kitty – I know it's funny right? It's *gazzy* – it's from Anne *Frank?* That's her diary, did you ever read that book?

BLANCHE. *(The whole thing is too much for her.)* Uh.

LILY. She kept a *diary?*

[STOP]

(She forgets what she was saying. She jingles her bangles. Beat.)

LILY. So-whatevah. *(resuming her checklist)* Do you know // how to

BLANCHE. Forgive me but I thought I had this job already.

(beat)

LILY. What-h.

BLANCHE. This feels like an interview.

(beat)

LILY. *(indignant)* Well I thought you would be Porto-*Rican!*

(*She pulls her gum out and makes shapes with it.*)

BLANCHE. Why'd you think that.

LILY. *(darts a look) Because we wanted a Porto-RICAN-h.*

(*She pops the gum back in her mouth.*)

BLANCHE. *I'm confused.*

LILY. I don't think this is gonna work out, lemme call you a car service.

(*She goes to the phone, dials.*)

BLANCHE. But I have all my luggage with me.

LILY. Wheh do you live.

BLANCHE. *(panicked) Don't do that.*

LILY. I have a carry thing *(into phone)* Always Available? I need a cahr.

BLANCHE. Please don't call me a cab // I don't

LILY. Do you want to take the train?

BLANCHE. *(We can see the despair.)* I'd...prefer. I. I don't have anywhere to *go.*

LILY. I'm more comfortable around Porto-Ricans. *(into phone)* Hello?

BLANCHE. LISTEN. I don't have anywhere to *go* and I'm tired, can't you just try me // out

LILY. *(into phone)* 929 Ocean Parkway, it's between –

(**BLANCHE** *grabs the phone, hangs it up.*)

BLANCHE. *(verging on tears)* I DON'T HAVE ANYWHERE TO GO!

[STOP]

LILY. Ya giving me a headeeche.

(*beat*)

BLANCHE. *(manages a smile)* Sorry.

(*beat*)

LILY. Ya meeking me very nervous-h.

BLANCHE. I'm – sorry. I'm...

(BLANCHE straightens up a few things to palliate – she assumes the comportment of some housekeeper LILY may have seen on television; she plasters on a smile. LILY, vaguely soothed, produces a nail file.)

LILY. *(files her nails; bright)* It's just I had Porto-Ricans my whole life, as maids? My mother had a Porto-Rican maid? and then when I was a little girl I had a maid called Anna Maria. She took care of me; I loved hah. she taught me *Spanish?* she took me to the *park,* and pushed me on the swing – *ella me decia. "Lily tú eres un angel, y tu pelo es de ceda // te quiero como mi hija*

BLANCHE. *Yo-tambien-te-puedo-mecer-en-el-columpio-vamos-al-parque-AHORA-MISMO!!*

(beat)

LILY. *(shocked, ecstatic, drops nail file) TU HABLAS ESPAÑOL!!!!!*

BLANCHE. (I studied languages)

LILY. *Do you want a piece a gum? //*

BLANCHE. *Gracias!*

(They chew gum and look at each other.)

LILY. I've been chewing this same gum for three days.

BLANCHE. That's a lot of gum.

LILY. *(quick)* It is? No it's not because it's just one piece. I been *chewin* it fa three days. *Heeeee.* I *love* gum, you know what I like, charms blow pops. OH MY GAWD. I used to get in so much *trouble?* in my *math* class? Oh my od-gay the *rabbi?* HEEEEEEE. because you're not allowed to chew gum? and he caught me? and I was gonna swallow it and I didn't? and he stuck it in my HAIH!!! *Ha ha ha ha ha.* Oh my goawd he was SO. SICK.

BLANCHE. Did //

LILY. Rabbi-Lerner-he's-SICK-oh-my-god-I-LOVE-him.

BLANCHE. You're in school. //

LILY. Me no I quit //

BLANCHE. You // did?

LILY. Lastchyee, because I got married. I wanted to stay but my mother told me quit. Anyway I had a lot of planning with the wedding and everything.

BLANCHE. *(pretending it's all normal)* How long have you been married?

LILY. I had a long engagement.

BLANCHE. How long?

LILY. Three years.

BLANCHE. Wow

LILY. I was twelve!

(beat)

BLANCHE. When you – got *engaged?*

LILY. *(filing nails)* Ye.

BLANCHE. *(incredulous)* You're *fifteen?*

LILY. Seventeen Well I'm gonna be My birthday's next week.

BLANCHE. But you said three years.

LILY. (I mis-did the math) We're goinna tavern on the *green!*

BLANCHE. That's quite a young age to be married.

LILY. What? Yeah. No. But I'm mature. *(contemplative)* I matured very fast starting when I was ten? I'm more matured since then, I was ten then I was a kid, I'm more matured now.

BLANCHE. Is that some kind of religious custom? To get married so young?

LILY. We're Jewish.

BLANCHE. You don't look Jewish.

LILY. How do I look?

BLANCHE. Middle Eastern.

(beat)

LILY. *(perplexed and annoyed)* Middle *Eastin!!??*

BLANCHE. You have Middle Eastern features. You know Dark Features?

LILY. *(squinting in disbelief)* I'm *tan*. I went to *Aruba?* //

BLANCHE. Not your complexion, your features.

LILY. I look *white*.

BLANCHE. Not to me.

LILY. *(indignant)* What do you mean not to you, *look at me* //

BLANCHE. I'm lookin.

(A brief staring contest.)

LILY. *(sheepish)* Well my family *they* are…I think from…the Middle East.

(beat)

BLANCHE. Where? //

LILY. *Aduknow the Middle East somewheh!*

BLANCHE. You don't know where?

(beat)

LILY. I think Syria.

BLANCHE. I didn't know there were Syrian // Jews.

LILY. But we're all *white*.

BLANCHE. Well technically you *aren't* white if // you

LILY. I tan easy? I have melanin in my skin?

(Beat. Then playing along.)

BLANCHE. *That's a nice tan.*

LILY. I'm peeling! *(She gleefully peels a huge rectangle of skin off her arm.)*

BLANCHE. *(horrified)* You should use lotion for that!

LILY. *I use!* //

BLANCHE. Black people use cocoa butter, that's why we don't get any wrinkles //

LILY. (I'm getting // wrinkles)

BLANCHE. You know that expression "black don't crack"?

LILY. No.

BLANCHE. That's where that's from.

LILY. You don't have any wrinkles.

BLANCHE. I know and I'm forty-three.

LILY. *(grabbing onto the sofa)* HEEEE. THAT'S FREAKIN OLD.

BLANCHE. *(disconcerted)* It's not *that* old.

LILY. (But-you-don't-look-it.)

BLANCHE. *(pridefully)* "Black don't crack."

LILY. Cocoa butter.

BLANCHE. And you're *not* getting // *wrinkles*

LILY. And your skin loses collagen That's what happens when you get old.

BLANCHE. Not you, you got great skin.

LILY. Your skin loses elastin, that's what happens, it's called "elastin." *(She goes up to the mirror and examines her "wrinkles" while speaking.)* So when people come to my house I want things to appear a certain way, like I want everything to be spotless – you see how everything is white that's how I want things to be Stunning stunning *white* //

BLANCHE. Does this mean I have // the job?

LILY. And we have a bucket of paint in every room So if things start to get dirty like if there's spots? like on the walls? or if you have nothing to do and there's down time you *repaint* ok?

BLANCHE. *(sigh of relief) Thank you.*

LILY. Can I call you Anna Maria?

BLANCHE. Why? //

LILY. I just like that name //

BLANCHE. I was hoping you'd call me Ms. Nesbitt //

LILY. *Who's that?* //

BLANCHE. Me.

   (beat)

LILY. I-kinda-hoped-I-could-call-you-Anna-Maria (is-that-*okaaaay*-I-feel-//-*baaaad*)

BLANCHE. I // kinda

LILY. *(regressing)* Anna-Maria-you're-so-nice-Anna-MARIA.

> *(She hugs* **BLANCHE***. She claps a tiny clap.)*
>
> *(beat)*

BLANCHE. Where's my room?

LILY. (cheerful*).* It's in the basement!

BLANCHE. And it's safe?

LILY. *(wide-eyed cheer)* We took the asbestos out of the *ceiling*!

BLANCHE. Oh // good (?)

LILY. There's an alarm //

BLANCHE. Ok.

LILY. (Could you not track // dirt?)

BLANCHE. (I'll take these // off)

LILY. *(single breath)* When you're finished unpacking you
can dustbust The kitchen's just around theh? you turn
right and it's right there ok? I'm gonna get a facial
here's my cell if you need it Oh wait I don't have a
pen.

BLANCHE. *(fear)* And I have the job right?

LILY. *(scrunches her face in the mirror)* (I'm losing elastin.)

BLANCHE. (You look // fine)

LILY. OOLIE! I'm going to be late for my manicuah //

BLANCHE. *Ok.*

LILY. *(frantically grabbing her things)* Down the stairs and the
first door on your left That's your room.

BLANCHE. Down // the –

LILY. No second //

BLANCHE. What //

LILY. Door //

BLANCHE. On my left? //

LILY. *No right.*

> *(***BLANCHE*** *descends the stairs, hauling her heavy lug-
> gage with her.)*

LILY. *(cont.)* *(chatters away in Spanglish after her)* Oh and be careful, the steps Let me show you It's very steep. *(Spanish, speaks quickly)* *Todavía estamos trabajando Anna Maria la luz está a tu derecha* *(runs after her)* Switch the alarm off, *cuidado Anna Maria* careful don't fall... ANNA MARIA!!!!

(She looks after BLANCHE descending the stairs, her eyes glowing preternaturally.)

(Arabic music cuts in, blasting.)

3.

(**JOJO** *and* **IKE**)

(*They're both in fishing gear.*)

(*Both wear jojo jeans.*)

(**IKE** *has a button that reads: "I like Ike."*)

(**LILY** *is carrying an enormous fish that's nearly twice her size and weight.*)

(**BLANCHE** *is in the periphery, repainting the walls with a roller.*)

IKE. You put it right on the grill //

LILY. With the bones?

JOJO. *(points)* Don't debone // it

LILY. Ert.

IKE. Grilled whole fish you never had that It's // unreal

LILY. (I nevah had // that)

JOJO. That's what gives it flava.

LILY. I never cooked fish.

JOJO. You put lemon You put salt You put garlic //

IKE. You put fresh oregano //

JOJO. Mint //

IKE. No // mint

JOJO. MY FATHER PUT // MINT

IKE. YOU DON'T PUT MINT!

(*They roughhouse for a few seconds.*)

(*It ends just as suddenly as it started.*)

LILY. I'm taking lessons, cooking lessons, at the école, we're still on vegetables //

IKE. Gimmethebosses //

LILY. There's six kinds a // dice

IKE. *(kissing her paternally)* (Gimmethebosses // gimmethebosses)

LILY. No seven, brunoise, something a "m"? Lemme // get my

IKE. ALRIGHTAREADY

LILY. What?!

IKE. WE'RE // HUNGRY

LILY. ARAAAIGHT!

> *[STOP]*

LILY. (Ooof)

> (**LILY** *exits, galled, lugging the huge fish.*)
>
> *[STOP]*
>
> (*The energy in the room shifts completely, becomes hyper-macho.*)
>
> (*Tableau*)

JOJO. She p.g.? //

IKE. *(makes a muscle)* Workin on it //

JOJO. Honeymoon? //

IKE. Feel //

JOJO. You're working out?

IKE. I joined the gym, gold's, I work out six days a week //

JOJO. I hired a trainer //

IKE. I run five miles a // day

JOJO. I run six //

IKE. I do crunches //

JOJO. I do squats //

IKE. *(pointing finger) You stretch?*

JOJO. I do bowflex //

IKE. *You wanna hurt your back?!* //

JOJO. *(points)* (Don't point).

> (*beat*)
>
> (**IKE** *jogs in place.*)

IKE. I'm in training.

JOJO. You gotta stretch the muscles.

IKE. I'm in pretty good shape // guy, my

JOJO. (Bowflex.)

IKE. age, look at Abie,

JOJO. Abie *yeah //* but

IKE. *(stops jogging)* Look at my stomach Jo, *flat //*

> *(He lifts his shirt.* **JOJO**, *in examining his stomach, punches it.)*

IKE. DID I SAY PUNCH?

> *[STOP]*

JOJO. (Good definition)

IKE. Flat //

JOJO. *(belated double take)* (Wait-Abie-who?)

IKE. *(strikes an Atlas pose)* Feel. //

JOJO. Whaddayouon*steroids?*

IKE. *(Atlas pose two)* Creatine.

JOJO. That's bad fa ya kidneys You want *kidney stones?*

IKE. *I don't got kidney stones ya douchebag //*

JOJO. *DOUCHEBAG //*

> *(Smack. Headlock. They get in Blanche's way.)*

IKE. Uncle.

JOJO. *NO!*

IKE. I'll break ya fuckin neck.

BLANCHE. (I'll move.)

> *(They fight, alternating putting each other in headlocks; it's quite stylized.)*

> *(***BLANCHE** *rolls her eyes.)*

JOJO. UNCLE!

> *(***IKE** *lets him out of the headlock.)*

IKE. Power.

JOJO. Now my neck hurts //

IKE. Name of the game *(to Kitty)* Hiiiiiiiiiiieeeeeeeeeee Kiiitty!

> *[STOP]*

> *(Energy in the room shifts again completely. a hyperreal business meeting.)*

JOJO. I'm hungry //

IKE. *(shift) Alright let's talk business.* //

JOJO. *Alright* (lemme get my // pad)

IKE. *Shoof.* outsourcing //

JOJO. Tawk.

IKE. We're at a time of expansion We need to leverage our capabilities Increase our profit margin //

JOJO. I // already

IKE. I know you don't wanna do // it but

JOJO. And then we gotta bring more *people* in, I don't // wanna

IKE. LISTEN TA MAY – We expand the market, pr, advertising //

JOJO. No –

IKE. (plus with decreasing the labor // costs)

JOJO. (It's-not-actually-so-much-cheaper-I-saw-the-spreadsheet.)

IKE. LISTEN TA MAY!

JOJO. I don't want no sweatshops, I'm not into that, *(He flexes some muscle.)* Ibe.

IKE. They're not sweatshops,

JOJO. (I'm starving // where's the fish?)

IKE. These people need work, they're dropping like *flies,* they're being barbecued *alive* they NEED WORK //

JOJO. I //

IKE. You wanna be a nike You wanna be a godiva chocolate?

JOJO. *(points)* Jojo jeans!

IKE. Jojo JEANS //

JOJO. *(moves to sofa)* And they got *sweatshops.*

IKE. (Who)

JOJO. Nike, godiva, child *labor* //

IKE. My *grammotha* worked in child labor she freakin *oved-it-lay* //

JOJO. *CA-AN //*

IKE. "*CA-AN*" in a candy factory They gave her free candy bars //

JOJO. We already have a sizable profit margin

IKE. What about our *skill set?*

JOJO. I //

IKE. We can leverage our capabilities CA-AN, Take it to the next level, we can be like a diesel, a levi's, a lee jeans (where's Brooke // Shields)

JOJO. I //

IKE. (Marky Mark The girl with the reversible mole) *not* this second-tier nonsense – if that's what you want fine I want MOAH!

JOJO. I want more // too.

IKE. *(practically edging him off the sofa)* No cause you're lazy // *move*

JOJO. I'm // not

IKE. Spoiled bastard if (MOVE) if // you

JOJO. I'M NOT SPOILED //

IKE. SHADDAP (if-your-father-didn't-have-money-you'd-be-scraping-the-gutters-with-the-back-of-your-throat) //

JOJO. *What //*

IKE. SHADDAP (you're-too-lazy-to-even-understand-the-shit-life-you'd-have-if-you-weren't-so-spoiled) *That's* corruption //

JOJO. *I'm* corrupt? //

IKE. That's *repreHENsible* //

JOJO. I'M //

IKE. (You're-sitting-on-your-blackberry) // REPREHEN-SIBLE do

JOJO. (Wheh) //

IKE. you realize how much you have to work with Your skill-set? Where's your ambition, where's your fire? – I'm like Vesuvius I'm like Magic Johnson I shoot hoops I have winged feet //

JOJO. I work my ass off. I *started* this company it's MY company //

IKE. ARE. YOU. IN?

(pause)

JOJO. You treat me like shit.

I'm your partner.

(pause)

IKE. I love you like a brother; you know that.

(beat)

JOJO. Yeah yeah.

(pause)

IKE. *(puts his arm around him)* Remember we picked up non-Jewish girls together?

JOJO. *(fond reminiscence)* The chick with bad teeth?

IKE. (deltoids, traps, rhomboids)

JOJO. Fucked up teeth is hot...

(beat)

IKE. Now we're *arried-may* //

JOJO. (She p.g. yet?)

IKE. I *told* // you

JOJO. "Be fruitful and // multiply"

IKE. I want ten // kids

JOJO. KILL THE PALE-FREAKIN-STINIANS //

IKE. (oneafteranothah-boom-boom-//-boom.)

JOJO. *(quick)* I says ta-hah. "YOUR BRA DON'T EVEN FIT-H" //

IKE. Who //

JOJO. *(quick)* She goes "I can't afford no bra" I go "I'll slip you twenty bucks if you show me your ass."

IKE. HA HA //

JOJO. HA HAHAHAH.

[STOP]

JOJO. *(beat; concession)* Arite //

IKE. YES?

JOJO. *(a little lost, abstracted)* I don't know what I'm doing.

IKE. *(preening happily)* Cuz I'm alpha, cuz what I say goes buddy

JOJO. *(violent)* BULLSHIT!

IKE. Alpha and the beta, the beginning and the end.

JOJO. (Omega.)

IKE. Who's got the power.

JOJO. *(regretting everything)* (I'm starved.)

IKE. *(posing in the mirror)* My arms are like *pistons.*

4.

(SHELLY *and* LILY)

(*They wear fila luxe tracksuits. Headbands too. Makeup: perfect.* LILY *is stretching her calves.* BLANCHE *is dusting inconspicuously in the periphery.*)

SHELLY. I used to get v's but now I do moons //

LILY. I have a French manicuah //

SHELLY. You go to linear nails? //

LILY. No I used to go theh.

SHELLY. With who Olga?

LILY. I don't go there // anymore.

SHELLY. Was she fat?

LILY. I go to Ana Orsini.

SHELLY. I used to go there.

[STOP]

LILY. I have a French manicuah.

(*shows her*)

SHELLY. Heeeee. Stunning.

LILY. Let me see your v's.

SHELLY. Moons.

LILY. I love // it-h

BLANCHE. Where's the pledge?

LILY. What.

BLANCHE. I'm dusting.

SHELLY. You use pledge? It gives you waxy buildup.

[STOP]

LILY. I thought //

SHELLY. (*harsh blame*) You use pledge??

LILY. (*meek*) Ye.

SHELLY. (*to* BLANCHE) LISTEN TA MAY. you don't use that, you wanna ruin all the furnitcha it's brand-new furnitcha very expensivo mucho dinero, you wanna ruin this?

(BLANCHE shakes her head.)

SHELLY. You don't use that on the furniture. *(to* **LILY***)* Did you tell her about the floors?

LILY. I //

SHELLY. *(to* **BLANCHE***; eyeing her suspiciously)* You be careful with the floors araight?

BLANCHE. *(restraint but it's difficult)* What would you have me use.

SHELLY. *I can't remembah* it's this stuff // *(snap, snap)*

LILY. Anna // Maria

SHELLY. *What's the freakin name? (disproportionately angry) I CAN'T REMEMBAH. (snap, snap) It's much bettah.*

[STOP]

BLANCHE. Well //

SHELLY. I'll have you call my girl My girl is very good She'll give you the name.

LILY. *(after an uncomfortable spell)* Did you get the invitation // for

SHELLY. Oh and I'm pregnant-h.

(beat)

LILY. *You're* –

SHELLY. The-baby's-fine-no-disfigurement-I-got-the-ultra-sound-Tuesday.

LILY. HEEEEEE. SHEL // CONGRATS

SHELLY. (I saw a little hand I saw little feet.)

LILY. When did // you

SHELLY. I'm done with the first trimester they tell you not to tell anyone before that, I can still do exercise, speedwalking aerobics. *am I glowing?* //

LILY. Ye //

SHELLY. (Badminton.)

(beat)

SHELLY. It's nice being pregnant just to glow.

LILY. *(twirling her hair)* Did you tell Jo?

SHELLY. Yeah I mean no, I'll tell him, ca-an. Let's speed-walk.

(beat)

LILY. Do I?

SHELLY. What.

LILY. Glow.

(beat)

SHELLY. *(rhetorical)* Are *you* pregnant?

(**SHELLY** *smiles a freakishly wide, teasing smile at* **LILY**; *pokes at her stomach.*)

(**BLANCHE** *looks disdainfully at* **SHELLY**. **SHELLY** *stares her down.* **BLANCHE** *goes back to dusting, feigning interest in her dumb job.*)

LILY. Let's speedwalk I have my thing.

(**SHELLY** *makes to leave. Hawk-like, she watches* **BLANCHE**, *her mouth curled into a snarl.*)

SHELLY. Shoof haddie.

(**LILY** *looks up at* **SHELLY** *who is still fixed on* **BLANCHE**.)

SHOOFIE.

(**LILY** *jolts, looks to* **SHELLY** *and then* **BLANCHE**.)

(**BLANCHE** *freezes a moment, then slowly pivots to see if she's being watched.*)

(**SHELLY** *casually fingers the furniture for dust.*)

(looks out casually) Ooday ooyay ink-thay ee-shay eels-stay?

(**BLANCHE** *stops for a moment;* **LILY** *doesn't get it on the first try.*)

LILY. Uht-way?

SHELLY. Do you *think* she *eels-stay?*

LILY. *(slightly embarrassed)* I don't ow-knay.

SHELLY. SHOOFIE. *(pause)* My *last* aid-may ole-stay ings-thay.

(**LILY** *looks at her.*)

(whispers loudly) And she wasn't an *igger-nay.*

(**BLANCHE** *freezes.*)

LILY. *(deeply uncomfortable)* When are we going already?

SHELLY. *Iggers-nay eel-stay.*

5.

(IKE and LILY.)

(The master bedroom, night.)

(IKE does pushups on the floor. LILY watches him, bored.)

IKE. Eighteen Nineteen.

LILY. She needs it to be off the books she said.

IKE. Twenny (sit-on-me) twenny-one.

(She gets on his back while he does pushups.)

LILY. She doesn't want to pay taxes.

IKE. So.

LILY. So she doesn't want a check, anyways I need money.

IKE. Don't I give you money?

LILY. I had to pay the gardener.

IKE. Twenny-seven.

LILY. And Frieda's shower, I had to get her // a present

IKE. You don't have enough money?

LILY. I //

IKE. Look at this house, you don't like this house?

LILY. (No I like it.)

IKE. Those are dolomite floors.

LILY. Shelly has a credit card.

IKE. Use Shelly's I'll give you the money.

(LILY stands.)

LILY. Could I have my own bank account?

IKE. We have a bank account (thirty-six).

LILY. My name's not on it.

IKE. Why do you need your name on everything.

LILY. My mother says that she never heard of a husband // who won't

IKE. Your mother should mind her own business.

LILY. DON'T TURN ME AGAINST MY FAMILY.

[STOP]

(More pushups. She brushes her hair and cries.)

IKE. What the hell is wrong with you.

LILY. Aduknow.

IKE. Why are you *crying?*

LILY. I cry better than I speak.

IKE. Who says?

LILY. YOU.

(Beat. He produces cash.)

IKE. You need more I'll give you more

LILY. I always need moah.

IKE. You buy gadgets.

LILY. *(gravitas)* I need gadgets.

IKE. No one // needs

LILY. You don't know what I need.

*(**IKE** stands.)*

IKE. I don't know what you need?

(He grabs her. They kiss. It's not that sexy.)

That's a good girl.

(She looks up at him with her big, watery eyes. She chews her gum. She brushes her hair.)

LILY. I'm bohed.

IKE. Your hair smells nice.

LILY. *(cheered)* There's no flakes *right-h?*

IKE. Who's my little girl.

LILY. Me.

IKE. *(stroking her cheek)* We'll talk about getting you a credit card.

LILY. *(She sits on his lap.)* Also I want to take acting lessons.

IKE. You're already taking // lessons

LILY. At the école but that's cooking.

(pause)

IKE. I thought you wanted a family.

LILY. I can have // both

IKE. Because I want to have a family I thought that was clear.

(*beat*)

LILY. Maybe we // could

IKE. And I want it now //

LILY. But //

IKE. NOW I WANT IT NOW!

(*He kisses her violently, starts tearing off her clothes.* **BLANCHE** *enters with laundry.*)

BLANCHE. (*Ooh I'll come back.*)

(**BLANCHE** *exits.* **LILY** *pulls away.*)

(*long pause*)

LILY. I got fitted for a diaphragm.

(*pause*)

IKE. Where is it.

(*beat*)

LILY. In the draw.

IKE. Get it.

LILY. I just thought in // case

IKE. GET IT.

(*Pause. She goes to the drawer.*)

IKE. Flush it.

LILY. But I…I just got it.

(*Beat. He stares her down. She exits and returns.*)

IKE. (*sweet*) I didn't hear a flush.

LILY. You wanna check?

IKE. Don't use that tone with me.

(*Chews her gum. Pops.*)

LILY. We nevah do anything.

IKE. We just got back from Aruba.

LILY. I don't like being alone.

IKE. *(gleeful)* You're not alone – you got the ghost!

LILY. You shouldn't have told me about that.

IKE. *(teasing)* Awwwwwwww you scared of the ghost?

LILY. It's not funny //

IKE. BOO //

LILY. AAAAAAH

(*She screams, he laughs. Stop.*)

IKE. Honey there's no such thing as ghosts; don't be a dumbell.

(*He ruffles her hair.*)

LILY. You told me the real estate guy said it was haunted

IKE. You gonna listen to some real estate guy?

LILY. You said you believed it.

IKE. *(gently, playful)* Calm down.

LILY. I saw it. I saw it the other day. *(beat)* I saw a face.

(**IKE** *looks at her, smiling curiously.*)

IKE. You saw a ghost?

(*beat*)

LILY. In the living room – the other day.

(*beat*)

IKE. Honey, you're just seeing things.

LILY. *(increasingly upset, a child's nightmare)* It was looking right at me.

(*He looks at her – he's a bit spooked.*)

IKE. You saw somm?

LILY. The real estate guy told you – I'm not making // it up

IKE. Ok ok Look at me.

LILY. I saw a face.

IKE. Honey look at me.

(**LILY** *looks at him.*)

IKE. You think a ghost is gonna mess witchu when you got me protecting you?

LILY. *(sad)* When are you leaving?

IKE. China? I told you, Thursday.

LILY. Are you going to be gone for my birthday?

IKE. I leave right after.

LILY. How long will you be gone?

IKE. A few weeks.

LILY. Can I come?

IKE. Business.

(*Pause. She goes to mirror, brushes her hair.*)

LILY. *I'm not a dumbbell.*

(*beat*)

IKE. Who's my little girl?

(*no answer*)

(*seducing her*)

Daddy just has to be gone a little while and then he'll be home to take care of his baby.

(*pause*)

LILY. *(vulnerable)* I. I get panic attacks.

IKE. *(making fun of her)* "I get panic attacks."

(*beat*)

LILY. *(shocked by his cruelty)* It's not funny.

IKE. *(thinks this is funny)* AlrightAlright.

(*beat*)

LILY. I want to go with you.

IKE. Who's my little gadget?

LILY. *(frightened)* Don't leave.

IKE. Gimmethebosses.

6.

(**BLANCHE** *and* **IKE**)

(*The kitchen. Morning.*)

(**BLANCHE** *has just made a pot of coffee, she's playing waitress.* **IKE** *is eating – or slurping giant mouthfuls of cereal, alternating with drinking his creatine shake.*)

BLANCHE. Refill? //

IKE. Just a few things, you come in, not a big deal I was thinking Sunday //

BLANCHE. That's my day off.

IKE. (Get me some milk.)

BLANCHE. Right // but

IKE. Yeah but I need you to do it Sunday see because I have stuff going on so it has to be Sunday It's no big thing.

BLANCHE. You want me to come into your office //

IKE. Cuz we're moving, Hong Kong, stuff What's this?

BLANCHE. What? Oh. Soy milk.

IKE. I want regular milk.

BLANCHE. But have you tried // soy?

IKE. (*slams down milk, it spills*) GET RID OF IT.

[STOP]

BLANCHE. But it's // very

IKE. (*petulant, shouting*) I WANT MILK REGULAH MILK.

[STOP]

IKE. Here's a sponge //

BLANCHE. I'll // clean it

IKE. (Where's-the-splenda-we-got-splenda?) //

BLANCHE. I //

IKE. (*bright*) So this Sunday aright.

BLANCHE. Where?

IKE. The warehouse? It's in Jersey, Hoboken, I'll give you carfare I'll give you twenny bucks Don' worry about nuthin //

BLANCHE. This is making me uncomfortable. //

IKE. *(Where's-the-splenda?)* //

BLANCHE. Because. I, uh. I really don't clean offices?

IKE. You //

BLANCHE. Or. Well that's not what I was *hired* to do.

> *(He gives her a dirty look. Downs some creatine.)*
>
> *(increasingly nervous)* And. And I…The *boundaries?* *(beat)* Do you see what I mean?

IKE. *(strained cheer)* An awffice is a house but with file cabinets.

BLANCHE. But. It isn't *really* a house.

IKE. Pretend it's a house.

BLANCHE. But //

IKE. *(bright)* Just pretend.

BLANCHE. Maybe we could organize it for later in // the week

IKE. *(violent)* I'M-ASKING-YOU-TO-DO-ONE-THING!

> **(BLANCHE,** *frightened, reflexively tries to shield herself.* **IKE** *looks at her, completely unaware of his effect on her. Beat.)*

IKE. Whatsamatta?

BLANCHE. I – //

IKE. BOO!

BLANCHE. *(terrified)* AHHHHHH!

IKE. *(delighted)* I scahe ya? AH HAHAH.

> **(BLANCHE** *makes a feeble attempt to laugh along with him.)*

IKE. Just do this for me, you're doing this for me *(I'll give you twenny bucks) What kinda music izzat?*

BLANCHE. Rachmaninoff.

IKE. It's giving me a headache BAH BAH BAH.

> **(BLANCHE** *shuts it off.)*

BLANCHE. *(a concession; cleaning his spilled cereal)* I used to work in an office; I did bookkeeping.

IKE. Good girl //

BLANCHE. I did a lot of office // jobs

IKE. You're gonna clean this up I gotta go.

(*He gathers his things.*)

IKE. You could make a lot of money bookkeeping, why don't you do that?

BLANCHE. Capitalism, cubicles, it's not for me.

IKE. But if you got *skills* Your *skill*set?

BLANCHE. Offices make me claustrophobic.

IKE. *Awffices?*

BLANCHE. The whole system.

IKE. Whaddayou a *commie?*

BLANCHE. Commie? No, more, uh //

IKE. (*checks out her booty*) Commie //

BLANCHE. democratic socialist? anyway I resist labels //

IKE. (What are those, levi's?) //

BLANCHE. But the System wants to crush you.

IKE. "System"?

BLANCHE. The political truncheon? //

IKE. You got a good vocabulary.

BLANCHE. I got a PhD.

IKE. College, ye, not for me.

BLANCHE. I speak four languages.

(*beat*)

IKE. But there's only one language spoken in this world.

(*He looks right at her.*)

BLANCHE. Which is.

(*beat*)

IKE. Gold and Silver baby.
Money talks. (*beat*)
That's right.

[STOP]

BLANCHE. Are you still // hungry?

IKE. And I don't want you wearing no levi's, *listen ta may.*
I'll give you a closetful of jeans – the best – jojo jeans, a
closetful. HOT. The *best,* you *listenna-may.*

BLANCHE. I don't got a closet.

IKE. Wha?

BLANCHE. My room, I use a suitcase.

IKE. *(preening)* I'll get you a closet.

BLANCHE. *(irony)* (Oo-that'd-be-nice.) //

IKE. You like ya room? //

BLANCHE. *(tense smile)* Well-I feel-like-the-*walls*-are-closing-
in-on-me-but-*yeah.*

IKE. You could take somethin for that.

BLANCHE. *(finessing)* I'm a little claustrophobic aha // ha

IKE. *(a bit too loud)* YOU LIKE HIP-HOP!?

BLANCHE. *(jumps)* I *yeah* I I like Tupac.

IKE. *Who?*

BLANCHE. They shot him? //

IKE. To me it's // noise

BLANCHE. (And Jay-Z got gunned down in that // video?)

IKE. I like it but it's noise //

BLANCHE. Well.

    [STOP]

IKE. *(swaggering)* You're a hip-hopster.

BLANCHE. I like Sibelius best.

    (She watches him swagger. She doesn't know what to do.)

IKE. *("rapping")* the hip
the hop
the hip hip hippity hop
AND YOU DON'T STOP.
[STOP]

BLANCHE. Uh.

IKE. I know about hip-hop cause of my business, which is
fashion Denim You like denim?

BLANCHE. It's – versatile.

IKE. You dress nice.

BLANCHE. Thanks.

(BLANCHE cleans.)

IKE. No I'm serious yo.

(BLANCHE cleans. IKE struts over.)

Is that a hip-hop shirt?

BLANCHE. I don't know.

IKE. "FUBU. for us by us."

BLANCHE. Mm.

IKE. Like that.

BLANCHE. *(visibly uncomfortable)* Yeah.

IKE. Nice.

(beat)

BLANCHE. You like Sibelius?

IKE. You like me?

(stop)

(seductive) You like me?

(He grabs her around the waist from behind. She carefully disentangles herself.)

BLANCHE. I'll get the dustbuster.

(She exits.)

7.

(The night of **LILY***'s birthday.)*

(It's the middle of the night. **LILY** *has come home from her party. She holds a few helium balloons tied together. She can't sleep. She looks in the mirror.)*

*(***BLANCHE** *is reading by lamplight in the living room. She watches* **LILY***.)*

BLANCHE. How was the party.

LILY. I'm old.

BLANCHE. Nice balloons.

LILY. What are you reading?

BLANCHE. You wouldn't like this.

LILY. Could you read to me?

BLANCHE. It's theory.

LILY. What kinda theory? *(grabs the book)* I din know you liked to read.

BLANCHE. Cause I'm a maid?

LILY. Ye.

BLANCHE. "Ye"?

LILY. YE!?!? *(flipping through the book)* What kinda book is this?

BLANCHE. Semiotics (can I have that back?)

LILY. What's *semiotics-h*?

BLANCHE. The science of sign systems.

LILY. Why are you *reading* it?

> *(***LILY** *flips through it.)*

> *(deeply offended)* This is *retarded.*

BLANCHE. Well I have my degree in it. So. And I might have a teaching gig, I'm waiting to hear.

> *(***LILY** *just looks at her, waits for the punch line.)*

LILY. *(squinting)* What *degree?*

BLANCHE. *(getting excited)* I did my undergraduate work at Chicago? I studied lit with (well-minored-in-philosophy) but with Saul Bellow?

LILY. Saul –

BLANCHE. He won the nobel prize?

LILY. *Heeeee!*

BLANCHE. And Paul de *Man* all these *guys.* They're mostly dead now, but nice dead white guys. And I did graduate work at brown in semiotics or – well under the rubric of critical // theory

LILY. What's *brown?*

BLANCHE. A college.

LILY. Is it a black school?

BLANCHE. It's integrated.

LILY. With what?

(beat)

BLANCHE. *(confounded)* White people (?)

LILY. *(scrunching up her face; indignant)* So why's it called *brown?*

BLANCHE. I think we should avoid racial issues

LILY. *(winsome)* (I always avoid them) *So you went to college? That's so shaahp!*

BLANCHE. And I even had a thing with Cornel West; well it // wasn't –

LILY. Who //

BLANCHE. He used to send me these letters? like loveletters and shit and he's all frontin he's all "your eyes your hips" // And he's

LILY. Your teacher?

BLANCHE. He's like "I want to collapse you into the fold." I was like "*un*fold me."

LILY. ?

BLANCHE. *(quick)* Actually it's kinda ironic cuz I studied representations of the African American Domestic in Mass Media with him & here I am – but I luuuv irony.

LILY. If you went to college you can get a job –

BLANCHE. Well I need. I – I have to pay – my *loans.*

LILY. *(clapping)* And you're my maid?

BLANCHE. For the time being.

LILY. *(sad)* But I *don't want you to go.*

BLANCHE. But I might have this teaching job //

LILY. *(earnest)* But-you-clean-my-house-*stunning* //

BLANCHE. *(produces pack of gum)* Gum? //

LILY. *(Hee I love // dentyne.)*

BLANCHE. *(quick)* And if I get it I can pay back my loans and it might lead to a tenure position Which can lead to making speeches and my book'll come out and I could maybe be a pundit Write for *harper's* Start a blog –

LILY. Why couldn't you just get a teaching job to start with//

BLANCHE. *(defensive)* DO YOU KNOW HOW HARD IT IS TO GET A TEACHING JOB?! *(compensatorily girlish; quick)* A-ha-ha I mean – no-but-the-academy is so *cloistered* I've applied for – I mean I can not tell you how many jobs I've applied for –

LILY. Really?

BLANCHE. Oh I used reams of paper *reams* forests, whole *arbors*; but it's very white and it's hard as a black woman a lesbian I mean I like white guys *fine* but it's kind of a closed system and everyone wants to teach //

LILY. Why //

BLANCHE. Because what else are you gonna do with your worthless semiotics degree.!?!? *Aha-ha just kidding.* No but they love the whole ivory tower thing knowamsaaayin? Because you're insulated from the real world. *That's* the academy. They won't look at *reality.* And of course it's all worthless I mean really does anyone give a SHIT about synecdoche or Kant's epistemological turn? *No!* // And the academy

LILY. You want taffy?

BLANCHE. wants you to believe that the life of the mind, critical thinking, that this is *worth* something but – SURPRISE – it's just more hucksterism, another trick (yeah-gimme-a-taffy) "Oh *take* out two hundred grand in loans" (but it's all part of the capitalist // machinery)

LILY. *(proffering taffy)* What's synecdoche? //

BLANCHE. *(chews taffy, blithe)* But on the other hand people have *agency* //

LILY. (I like // taffy)

BLANCHE. It's like Helen Keller said "I am only one person but I'm still a person." //

LILY. (I thought she was mute) //

BLANCHE. (I'm paraphrasin) //

LILY. (Oh) //

BLANCHE. But it's the same shit over and over. Absolute power corrupts absolutely History repeats like a bad case a reflux. "History is a document of barbarism" //

LILY. Who said that? //

BLANCHE. (This-guy-who-wrote-his-major-works-on-toilet-paper-because-he-was-a-political-//-prisoner)

LILY. (We're almost out of toilet // paper)

BLANCHE. (It's on my // list)

LILY. (Double ply) //

BLANCHE. *Yo me preocupo de esto //* cálmate

LILY. Wait. you're-a-*lesbian*?

BLANCHE. What.

　　(beat)

LILY. *(a frisson)* I feel like I heard you say you're a ..."esbian-lay."

BLANCHE. *(eating a taffy)* Yeah.

LILY. Yeah you *are* or yeah you *said* it?

BLANCHE. *Yeah* I said it cuz *yeah* I *am* it.

LILY. You're an actual "lesbian"?

BLANCHE. *(indignant)* No. I'm an optical illusion //

LILY. But like. don't you think that like the *girl* is supposed to go with the *guy*?

BLANCHE. *(playing dumb)* Why's that.

    (beat)

LILY. *(as if Blanche is mentally handicapped)* Because the *man?* is *orientated* towards the *woman?*

BLANCHE. *Why?*

    (beat)

LILY. *(unbridled frustration)* BECAUSE THE *GIRL?* IS ORI-ENTATED? TOWARDS THE *GUY.*

BLANCHE. (Not this girl)

LILY. (Adumundahstan)

BLANCHE. *(only barely hiding her condescension)* Adrienne Rich wrote an essay. that said that *all* women are lesbians. And there's a thing called. "compulsory het-erosexuality"; and that first we're *all* dykes but it's the *system* that makes us straight.

LILY. What *system?*

BLANCHE. Forces of History Culture The usual vectors.

LILY. (Sounds like a dibeh) //

BLANCHE. (Well she aint.)

    (beat)

LILY. Girls are supposed to have kids and get *married.* That's life.

BLANCHE. *No.* That's *your* life.

LILY. Uhhhhh. Ya not very *bright-h* if you can't see what I'm saying?

BLANCHE. Uhhhhh. Actually I graduated phi beta kappa with a 3.94 gpa. Don't tell me I'm not *bright.*

    (pause)

LILY. I just don't agree with your lifestyle.

BLANCHE. Well it's not up for *consensus.*

    (Pause. **LILY** *takes another tack.)*

LILY. In the *bible?*

BLANCHE. *(dismissive)* Yeah what do you know about the bible?

LILY. Uhh. I read it like a *hundred* times!?

BLANCHE. Where?

LILY. *(vindication)* THE YESHIVAH!?!?

BLANCHE. (Yeah so you know the bible What do you know) //

LILY. *(blunt textbook sanctimony)* LESBIANS IS WRONG //

BLANCHE. (And they taught you grammar // too Nice)

LILY. And I know about sodom and gomorrah!

BLANCHE. What do you know?

LILY. They were *sodomites*!

BLANCHE. And.

LILY. And they had *sodomy ca-an*? And god said to Lot's wife not to look back and she looked back.

   (beat)

BLANCHE. Would you look back?

LILY. God said no.

   (pause)

BLANCHE. *(internal; faraway)* I would.

   (LILY looks at her.)

LILY. Fine but then you turn to a pillar of salt.

   (BLANCHE turns to LILY.)

BLANCHE. You ever hear of a lose-lose proposition?

   (beat)

BLANCHE. *(somewhat portentous)* No. Not yet. But you will.

   (silence)

LILY. I should go theh maybe.

BLANCHE. What?

LILY. College? But I gotta have kids.

BLANCHE. Have em later.

LILY. I can't, Ikey wants them //

BLANCHE. Get your // GED

LILY. And I'm really mad cause my diaphragm fit me good; and then he made me flush it down the toilet.

BLANCHE. Why'd he do that?

LILY. I *told* you, cause Ikey wants ten kids, he wants to start right now? But I'm mad cause it fit me good.

(pause)

LILY. *What.*

BLANCHE. What.

LILY. You're making a face.

(pause)

BLANCHE. *(forced polite smile)* Dear, I don't mean to get involved, but – aha ha – don't you think you're making some...*bad* choices? *(She smiles a goofy smile.)*

LILY. No.

BLANCHE. *(more forced smiling)* Oh – ok. *(overly genteel)* Ok, that's fine. Can I have my book back?

LILY. *(not ceding the book)* I'm not making bad choices.

BLANCHE. You're right, it's none of my // business

LILY. Why? I'm making bad choices – because – I'm having a *family?*

(beat)

BLANCHE. Sweetie it's...you're sixteen – you're a baby.

LILY. I'm *married.*

BLANCHE. Maybe that was a mistake?

LILY. My mother got married at my age. Was that a mistake?

BLANCHE. You're a teenager and you're married to a middle-aged man – and now you want to have *kids?* //

LILY. *(venom)* I'm not a *lesbian* I can *have* them.

(pause)

*(**BLANCHE** grabs her book.)*

BLANCHE. G'night.

LILY. *(stranded, upset)* So you're saying I // should

BLANCHE. I'm not saying *anything.*

*(**BLANCHE** gets her things together, turns off the light.)*

LILY. *(rudderless)* So I should – what – get a // *divorce?*

BLANCHE. Good night //

LILY. I. I – you think I made bad choices? // *Why?*

BLANCHE. Just don't throw your life on the rubbish heap alright?

LILY. I don't think *this* is a rubbish heap.

BLANCHE. *(gesturing to all the white stuff)* Honey you live in an *igloo!*

LILY. So do *you.*

BLANCHE. Look. I'm grateful to have // this

LILY. Grateful means you keep your mouth *shut.*

(beat)

BLANCHE. No. *grateful* means you help someone who's helped you. *(real feeling)* Now you helped me, didn't you, you got me this job. *(beat)* And I need this job. I *need* this job. *(beat)* So now I want to help you.

LILY. *(weakly)* My family helps me.

BLANCHE. Your Family.

LILY. Ye.

BLANCHE. Is that what you believe?

LILY. Yes, they help me.

BLANCHE. Help you.

*(She holds **LILY***'s face in her hands.)*

LILY. *(weaker)* Yes.

BLANCHE. That's what you believe?

*(**LILY** looks at **BLANCHE**; she's inexplicably and suddenly sad now. She nods yes weakly.)*

LILY. *(holding back tears)* Why? You think they…they don't *like* me?

[STOP]

*(In the STOP the tension builds and builds. Then **BLANCHE** very suddenly grabs **LILY** – tight. She's overcome with emotion here, a quantum leap in feeling, that she works to control over the following. This is desperate, urgent, compulsive – she's not in control of it.)*

BLANCHE. Listen to me.

> (*beat*)

> (*clamps down on emotion, laserlike*) You're inside of it. You're in the labyrinth I got the silk thread. Let me help you *navigate* it. [STOP] You could make yrself a whole other person. [STOP] Be whoever you need to be. [STOP] Don't be a victim.

> (**LILY** *is incredibly curious, and also very upset.* **IKE** *has entered down the stairs, wearing only pajama bottoms. He watches them, unseen.*)

IKE. (*to* **LILY**) What are you doing?

LILY. (*startled*) Oh. I //

IKE. Why are you still up.

> (*He notices she's been crying. He looks at* **BLANCHE** – *caught.*)

> (*long pause*)

LILY. We were talking.

IKE. Come to bed.

LILY. Good night.

BLANCHE. And happy birthday.

LILY. Don't forget to. Uh. Pick up that stuff from – that cleaners.

> (**BLANCHE** *smiles a taut smile.* **LILY** *goes upstairs.* **BLANCHE** *stands there.* **IKE** *glowers at her – it's dreadfully uncomfortable. Eventually he turns around and walks upstairs.* **BLANCHE** *is left, solitary, still.*)

8.

(**SHELLY** and **JOJO**'s house)

(They have **IKE** and **LILY** over for dinner.)

(They're eating pot roast with chopsticks.)

SHELLY. The tap water's not KOSHAH.

(beat)

IKE. WHAT?

SHELLY. The rabbi said there's *crustaceans* //

IKE. in the *tap* // water?

SHELLY. *micro*-crustaceans

JOJO. Lobsters – Crabs – *Micro* //

SHELLY. (to **LILY**) (Stop-playing-with-your-hands) //

JOJO. Only bottled water you // could drink

SHELLY. (to **JOJO**) You're not using your chopstick right.

JOJO. I'm using it // right.

SHELLY. You hold it between this finger and this finger not that // finger and this finger

JOJO. I'm holding it between this finger and // this finger

SHELLY. I said NOT that finger THIS finger.

[STOP]

(They eat in silence. **SHELLY** monitors **JOJO**.)

SHELLY. How's the baby situation?

(**IKE** looks at **LILY**.)

LILY. (Adunknow.)

(They eat.)

JOJO. *I'll tell you one thing, my kids are movin to Israel; they're moving to Israel and they're joining the freakin Israeli army.*

(**LILY** looks at him, then goes back to playing with her food, lost in thought and feeling deeply out of place. A beat.)

IKE. (bragging somewhat) You know what's not kosher?. Snickers bars.

(They eat.)

SHELLY. Snickers and m&m's.

*(**IKE** darts a look to **SHELLY**, scandalized.)*

IKE. HEEE!

(He covers his mouth.)

JOJO. And twix!

*(**SHELLY** looks over to **JOJO** dismissively.)*

SHELLY. Ca-an twix.

*(**SHELLY** goes back to eating.)*

LILY. You want your *kid* to be in the *army?*

JOJO. What?

SHELLY. Israeli

JOJO. *(hip-hop posturing)* Kill the palefreakin*stini*ans yo!

*(Beat. **LILY** just stares at him, disbelieving.)*

LILY. You're not even Israeli.

*(**IKE** puts down his fork, turns to her.)*

IKE. It's the Jewish *state.*

LILY. But we're Arabs.

SHELLY. *(makes a face)* We're not Arabs you ga*zz*case.

(beat)

LILY. Gramma speaks *Arabic.*

SHELLY. Ca-an she's a old lady.

(beat)

LILY. Well, would you kill your own relatives? Because that's
  // what

JOJO. WE'RE NOT PALESTINIANS IDIOT – ah

LILY. We're Ara – //

SHELLY. They're terrorists.

(beat)

SHELLY. *Finish your silvertip.*

(She picks up her chopsticks and eats.)

(pause)

LILY. *(quiet indignation)* We're Arabs //

SHELLY. We're *Jews* dibeh, you know what Jewish is?

LILY. We have melanin in our skin. We come from the Iberian *peninsula*.

(beat)

IKE. The *what*??

LILY. WE'RE SPANIARDS FROM THE IBERIAN PENIN-SULA.

(beat)

IKE. Where are you learning this?

LILY. Don't you know your own *history*? that's who you *are*.

IKE. *(sarcasm)* Oh, really, so who *am* I?

(Eyeballing her. A beat.)

LILY. There was an inquisition //

IKE. *Yeah.* and they murdered JEWS //

LILY. And then we moved to Syria and became Arabs //

JOJO. I //

IKE. Who's telling you this.

[STOP]

LILY. *(playing with her food)* We're not white //

IKE. Shut up.

(beat)

LILY. We're Iberian // people fr –

IKE. *(threat)* SHUT. UP.

(They eat. Long silence.)

JOJO. *(to SHELLY)* Did you get your passport?

*(**SHELLY** doesn't answer.)*

IKE. I like the roast.

SHELLY. Silvertip.

JOJO. *(his mouth full)* Tendah.

(They eat.)

LILY. What passport.

SHELLY. *(to* **JOJO***)* Don't play with that.

LILY. Where are you going?

SHELLY. China *dibeh.*

LILY. You're going?

(She looks at **IKE***. He doesn't look at her.)*

SHELLY. I wanna try kung pao steak. //

JOJO. IT'S NOT KOSHER I TOLD YOU!

SHELLY. I wanna try certain restaurants, I wanna show you my fodors.

LILY. *(to* **SHELLY***)* You're going to China?

SHELLY. *(to* **JOJO***)* Djousee my fodors?

JOJO. "Buddha's delight."

SHELLY. Oh I'm gonna miss my lessons at padegat Could you tell Gerard? Oh and how's your backhand, is your wrist bettah?

LILY. *(trance)* My...

(pause)

SHELLY. Your wrist?

IKE. Honey –

*(***IKE*** *touches* **LILY***'s shoulder – she pushes him off and quickly exits.)*

IKE. Whereyagoin?

(He goes after her.)

SHELLY. *(to* **JOJO***)* And I want a Mao suit.

JOJO. Aright.

IKE. WHERE YA GOIN?

SHELLY. *You get bargains //*

JOJO. ARIGHT.

SHELLY. *(to* **JOJO***, pointing at her book)* Look at my fodors, *I want that!!*

(loud music)

9.

(**LILY** *and* **BLANCHE**)

(*Morning, a few days later, the living room.*)

(**BLANCHE** *is looking out of the window, cleaning.* **LILY** *sits back on the sofa, listless & out of sorts.*)

BLANCHE. Look at that cloud, it's like those cathedrals. I'd love to see those glistening white domes and minarets wouldn't you?

LILY. You want gum?

BLANCHE. Rome, Istanbul, I don't know I'd like to travel.

LILY. I thought you lived in Paris.

BLANCHE. I...I did.

LILY. So didn't you see em // then?

BLANCHE. I loved jogging the perimeter of the Jardin du Luxembourg and sometimes the Bois de Boulogne but I got shin splints cause the ground was unpaved it had rocks and things (oh, I miss bell)

LILY. Who?

BLANCHE. hooks I told you about her She's a girl I'm friendly with she's like...well we were kind of close at one point.

LILY. Is she a philosopher?

BLANCHE. She doesn't believe in labels (Neither does my other friend Luce).

LILY. Who's //

BLANCHE. A feminist, this other girl I know from France? You seem out of sorts.

(*pause*)

(**BLANCHE** *peers out the window.*)

LILY. (*glum*) Did you get your teaching job? //

BLANCHE. "I like a nice view but I like to sit with my back to it." That's a line from a book.

(*beat*)

(BLANCHE *turns to see a rather enervated, depressed*
LILY.)

BLANCHE. What's wrong?

LILY. Headache.

BLANCHE. When's your tennis lesson?

LILY. You know any songs in Spanish?

BLANCHE. You gotta find something to do, Lily. Otherwise
you're gonna fester. "Lilies that fester smell far worse
than weeds." That's Shakespeaah.

(BLANCHE *produces aspirin, water, hands them to* LILY.
LILY *takes the aspirin and drinks the water down.*)

LILY. *(plays with some taffy, stretches it out)* Ikey's plane was
delayed He called Something with the propellah.

BLANCHE. How long's he gonna be gone?

LILY. Two weeks, he went to China.

BLANCHE. Hip hip.

LILY. *(sad)* He said not to come.

BLANCHE. Will the mice play //

LILY. Will you read to me? //

BLANCHE. *(giving in) Fine.*

LILY. Could I snuggle up on your lap?

BLANCHE. *No.*

LILY. *Please?*

BLANCHE. *Fine.*

LILY. *(vulgar command)* Play with my haih!

BLANCHE. *(minstrelsy) Yes Miss Daisy //*

LILY. *(holds up Blanche's purse) I like when you call me that. Zat
your bag?*

BLANCHE. *Uh huh.*

LILY. *stunning-h.*

(LILY *pushes* BLANCHE's *hand onto her head, and uses
her hand to play with her own hair – as if to train her –
then looks up admiringly.*)

BLANCHE. *(reads from Keats)* "Ode on a Grecian Urn."

LILY. Ert.

BLANCHE. What 'Ert'?

(More hand training. **BLANCHE** *reads.)*

BLANCHE. Thou still unravish'd bride of quietness,
Thou foster-child of Silence and slow Time,
Sylvan historian, who canst thus express
A flowery tale more sweetly // than our rhyme.

LILY. You have nice cuticles.

BLANCHE. What? Uh – Oh – I bite them. *(continues reading)*
What men or gods are these? What maidens loth?
What mad pursuit? What struggle // to escape?

LILY. *(speaking over her)* That's from nerves. Sometimes I
bite the inside of my cheeks – is that weeid?

*(***LILY*** *pulls a little talisman out of Blanche's purse.)*

BLANCHE. *(continues reading)* What struggle to escape?
What pipes and timbrels? What wild ecstasy? //

LILY. *(holds up talisman)* whatsat? //

BLANCHE. *(grabs it, shoves it back in)* Stop goin through my
things! I thought you wanted me to read.

LILY. I do. What's this from?

BLANCHE. Keats.

LILY. It's boring.

BLANCHE. O *please* //

LILY. Poems and things. *ERT.*

BLANCHE. It's not *boring.*

LILY. It makes me tired.

BLANCHE. Is beauty boring?

LILY. Yes.

BLANCHE. Is *life* // boring?

LILY. I bought a new stunning belt with gold *pieces.*

(exasperated pause)

BLANCHE. You know what? You have to develop your aes-
thetics.

LILY. *(abstracted) Why?*

BLANCHE. Cuz the apprehension of beauty is an essential part of being human, that's *why*. "Beauty is Truth, Truth Beauty"

LILY. I know. but beauty is *boring* – like I look at like a flower and I go. "Ye, petals, ca-an!"

BLANCHE. It's not just // petals!!

LILY. And plants – I hate them, I hate watering them, you get dirt all over the place from the water from when it leaks out and you track it on the floah!

(**BLANCHE** *stares at her in disbelief.*)

LILY. *(rifles through candy)* Hee, I love gummy worms, I get naushus from them but-h. I like souah. *(eats)* I like souah patch. I get naushus but-h.

(**BLANCHE** *stares at her.*)

LILY. *What.*

BLANCHE. Do you want me to read or not?

(pause)

BLANCHE. What pipes and timbrels? What // wild

LILY. Could you clean behind the refrigerator?

BLANCHE. *(slams down her book)* You have the *attention* span of an *aphid*.

LILY. Thehe's *mold!*

[STOP]

(**BLANCHE** *bolts up to clean, picks up a rag.*)

LILY. What's a aphid? //

BLANCHE. (Heard of a dictionary?) //

LILY. Tickle my arm! //

BLANCHE. *(throws down the rag) I gotta go on break //*

LILY. The whole day is your break.

BLANCHE. Excuse you?! //

LILY. You're lazy You don't do any work.

BLANCHE. Because you keep dragging me over to read you poems and play with your frizzy hair //

LILY. (I'm-using-hot-oil-treatments.) //

BLANCHE. I just want to get *by* – Is that alright?

LILY. I thought you said you wanted to help me.

BLANCHE. I just want to get by. Is that *ok* with you? Can I get *by*?

[*STOP*]

LILY. You have an attitude problem.

BLANCHE. *(thrown)* I have a *what*?

LILY. *(crossing her arms)* It's not workin out –

BLANCHE. Don't you know that ALL black people have an attitude problem.

LILY. *(ingenuous)* Yeah but why?

BLANCHE. *(minstrelsy)* Well, you know dat just how we are! druggies, welfare mothahs, Dat's just how it is for us black folk – *we sho don't know any betta!*

LILY. You don't have to be so whiney about everything. Oprah doesn't whine.

BLANCHE. You need to be *slapped* //

LILY. You leave grime on the bath // tile!

BLANCHE. *Where's Ike Turner when you need // him!*

LILY. Pack your // things

BLANCHE. And your damn husband needs to take anger management classes.

LILY. He has *mood* swings and I *love* him for his mood swings! And you're a very nasty *girl* //

BLANCHE. Actually I'm not a GIRL.

LILY. I //

BLANCHE. And I'm not YOUR girl, I'm my own *woman* and I kicked and bit and screamed and ripped people apart to BE that so do not FUCK. WITH ME.

[*STOP*]

(Sorry-I-don't-know-what-came-over-me.)

*(**LILY** is breathing rapidly, she's not well.)*

Are. Are you –

LILY. Could you get my ativan.

BLANCHE. Are you alright?

> (LILY *slumps, dizzy, over to the sofa, covers her face,* *breathes heavy. Almost a whimpering.* BLANCHE *runs* *to* LILY*'s purse, grabbing her ativan, gets her water, etc.)*
>
> *(pause)*

BLANCHE. I'm sorry. I didn't mean to //.

LILY. *(looks up; she's terrified) I don't want to be alone.*

> *(beat)*

BLANCHE. *(smiling kindly)* We're *all* alone sweetie.

LILY. I'm *not.*

BLANCHE. Ok.

LILY. I'm not alone.

> *(beat)*

BLANCHE. You can rest your head on my lap.

> (LILY *does.)*
>
> *(beat)*

LILY. Will you tickle my arm?

> (BLANCHE *tickles her arm.)*

LILY. You're not really fired *Anna Maria.*

BLANCHE. I know.

> *(She plays with* LILY*'s hair for a while.)*

LILY. Thank you.

BLANCHE. For what.

LILY. Taking me to get the pill.

> *(pause)*

BLANCHE. Are you takin em?

> (LILY *nods.)*

And you popped em out and put em in the midol bottle like I said?

> (LILY *nods.)*

BLANCHE. *(cont.)* Good girl.

(**BLANCHE** *squeezes her arm.*)

(pause)

LILY. Thank you. Blanche.

(**LILY** *looks up at her lovingly.*)

You have such a nice face.

BLANCHE. *(laughs; a little shy)* What?

LILY. You do, you have good bone structure.

BLANCHE. Well.

LILY. You have high cheekbones //

BLANCHE. Thanks //

LILY. Does that prevent you from sleeping in certain positions?

(beat)

BLANCHE. *(surprisingly flirtatious)* I'm adept at many positions.

(**LILY** *sits up.*)

LILY. *(panicked – defusing)* You-know-who-has-good-bone-structure-Iman.

(She turns away from **BLANCHE**.*)*

[STOP]

(**BLANCHE** *tickles her arm from behind.*)

Ha ha. *(then coyly serious)* No-no.

(**BLANCHE** *stops.* **BLANCHE** *starts again.*)

Ha ha. *(Beat)* No-no-no.

(She brushes off her arm.)

(**BLANCHE** *turns to go.*)

BLANCHE. I –

(**LILY**, *in one gesture, sweeps around, grabs* **BLANCHE**'s *arm, turns her around and kisses her passionately, fully on the mouth.*)

End Act One

ACT TWO

The Pleasure of the Text

1.

(BLANCHE and LILY)

(BLANCHE's room)

(Music playing softly in the background, maybe something 80s.)

(They're tasting wines. There's a bunch of wine bottles out – they're both slightly tipsy.)

(Their intimacy is significantly evolved here.)

BLANCHE. Swish.

(LILY swishes.)

Through the teeth. Slurp.

(LILY gargles.)

It's not Listerine, honey. Watch. comme ça.

(BLANCHE slurps.)

(LILY slurps.)

What do you feel?

LILY. Firmness?

BLANCHE. Are you asking me or telling me.

LILY. Aduknow!

BLANCHE. Feel it evaporate in your retronasal passage //

LILY. *(wine in mouth)* Ok //

BLANCHE. (No swallow first)

LILY. I taste...burnt match?

BLANCHE. Good //

LILY. (And grass?)

BLANCHE. What else?

LILY. Can we just drink?

BLANCHE. You don't want to get to drunk.

LILY. I do.

BLANCHE. The French don't drink to get drunk //

LILY. (I'm Jewish) *What's this?*

BLANCHE. Châteauneuf du pape.

LILY. S'it good?

BLANCHE. 1950 that's a great year This is an excellent vineyard –

LILY. It is?

BLANCHE. Microclimatic Small yields No this is *incroyable* ooh grrrrrrrl (here sniff).

(She does.)

LILY. It's…cheeky.

BLANCHE. *(laughing)* What's that mean?

LILY. I don't know.

BLANCHE. You're cheeky.

(A whiff of sexual tension; **BLANCHE** *pulls back.)*

BLANCHE. That's a '99 leroy.

LILY. Shoof.

BLANCHE. They're one of the great producers of white burgundy //

(She sniffs.)

LILY. You know so much //

BLANCHE. (Oak on the nose) I make it my business to know. If you make something your business, you know it inside out.

LILY. I know you inside out.

(beat)

BLANCHE. *(cynical laughter)* That's what you think.

LILY. *(playfully brazen)* That's what I *know.*

(pause)

BLANCHE. Don't you know it's dangerous to trust people you don't know very well.

LILY. I feel light.

(pause)

BLANCHE. You want something to hold on to, that's all. You haven't found yourself, that's why. You don't know who you are, you haven't found yourself.

LILY. *(drunken flirting)* Who am I?

(She gets close to her face.)

Who am I?

*(She kisses her; **BLANCHE** pulls away.)*

What.

BLANCHE. Nothing; you remind me of someone.

LILY. Did she love you?

(pause)

BLANCHE. Not like that.

(pause)

LILY. Because *I* love you.

[STOP]

BLANCHE. *No.*

LILY. *(almost weeping)* I *love* you //

BLANCHE. You – ha ha. Y – you're just a tadpole //

LILY. I'm not a tadpole! //

BLANCHE. *(shooing)* Swim away little fishie you're too young.

LILY. But //

BLANCHE. (Go find a nice Syrian girl // and)

LILY. NO.

BLANCHE. I am *forty-three.*

LILY. So? //

BLANCHE. So I'm not going to take advantage of a six-teen-//year-old girl.

LILY. (Seventeen) you're not taking // advant –

BLANCHE. *(resisting)* It's not *ethical* //

LILY. I know you like me.

BLANCHE. Once is ok, but that's it; I'm not embroiling you in this.

LILY. In *what?*

(beat)

What about Adrienne Rich //

BLANCHE. She's passé.

(beat)

LILY. *(assured)* I think you're in love with me.

(a shift)

BLANCHE. When's hubby comin back?

LILY. He's in the Orient.

BLANCHE. I know *that* but // when's he

LILY. *A few days.*

(pause)

BLANCHE. Let's just sit here with our little fluted glasses and chop it up alright?

LILY. Chop what up?

BLANCHE. Talk.

(**BLANCHE** *downs a glass of wine, pours herself another.*)

LILY. Where'd you grow up?

BLANCHE. Moved around.

LILY. No but – when you were adopted.

BLANCHE. I was twelve.

LILY. And // you

BLANCHE. And I moved to Philadelphia //

LILY. Liberty bell? //

BLANCHE. With the crack yeah //

LILY. And then you lived in the homeless shelter?

BLANCHE. *(regretting telling her this)* That was later.

(beat)

LILY. *(bright)* I never met anyone from a homeless shelter!!

BLANCHE. *(dry)* Yeah well – tick it off.

(She downs some wine.)

LILY. and were your parents nice? What were they like?

BLANCHE. *(frozen smile)* I don't want to talk about him.

LILY. Who?

BLANCHE. I mean them.

LILY. Why?

(pause)

BLANCHE. Cuz it's the past It's an illusion.

(beat)

LILY. But you said you have to know the past.

BLANCHE. Yeah but //

LILY. you said if you don't know history you become its victim – you're contradicting yourself.

BLANCHE. "I'm not contradictory. I am *dispersed.*" Roland Barthes.

LILY. Ooh I got a flash card fa him //

BLANCHE. keep up the flash cards.

(beat)

LILY. *(naifish curiosity)* What were their names?

BLANCHE. who?

LILY. your parents?

(Beat. Then wearily.)

BLANCHE. *(sighing)* Rich and Audrey.

LILY. "Rich and Audrey" //

BLANCHE. White //

LILY. "Audrey White" that's a pretty name //

BLANCHE. No. *They* were *white.*

LILY. what were they like?

(Beat. **BLANCHE** *doesn't look at her.)*

BLANCHE. I was a black kid raised by white people.

(**LILY** *looks at her, curious.* **BLANCHE** *doesn't answer.*)

LILY. Did you have black friends?

BLANCHE. *(staccato, taut)* Didn't have nuthin Kept to myself. Let's talk about summ else.

(*pause*)

LILY. Were your parents nice?

(*beat*)

BLANCHE. Will you stop *asking* // me that?

LILY. I'm // curious

BLANCHE. *(snaps at her)* NO they weren't nice they were fucking *horrible is that what you want to hear*?! Fingers on me middle a the night in my room night after night Think anyone did a goddam thing to stop it? "You're *black* You're a *woman* You're at the bottom of the *world*" Know how many times I heard that shit?!

(**LILY** *takes a sip of wine, discomfited. Long awkward pause.*)

BLANCHE. *(forcing a tiny smile)* So – so did you. Didja ever think about – girls before?

LILY. *(softening)* Not before this.

BLANCHE. Not even *once?*

(*beat*)

LILY. Well once.

[STOP]

BLANCHE. Ok-wait-let-me-get-comfortable

LILY. When I was in the dressing room //

BLANCHE. Where //

LILY. Loehmann's //

BLANCHE. *(blunt)* What's *loehmann's* //

LILY. (You get bras and coats) //

BLANCHE. Oh.

LILY. There's a public dressing room //

BLANCHE. *(swirling her wine)* They say a public dressing room is a dyke's business office //

LILY. (Really?) //

BLANCHE. (No).

LILY. So my mother used to take // me

BLANCHE. Loooooehmann's //

LILY. And I was really young, and I saw – you know; "that stuff."

(*beat*)

BLANCHE. "*Stuff*"?

LILY. That. Yeah.

BLANCHE. *(amused)* And you liked it.

LILY. Aduknow.

BLANCHE. Well *did* you or *didn't* you?

(*beat*)

LILY. I wasn't aware that I liked it? But…I think looking back?…Ye. //

BLANCHE. *(mock warning)* But don't look
back //

LILY. *What*?

BLANCHE. *(smiling at her inside joke)* Pillar of salt, etceteras –

LILY. Oh.

BLANCHE. But we'll *all* go to hell now WHEEEEEE //

LILY. I don't feel good //

BLANCHE. (It could be the sulfites Are you asthmatic?) //

LILY. I feel like I could fall.

BLANCHE. You're just drunk.

LILY. You're not.

BLANCHE. I drink all the time, It's the law of diminishing returns //

LILY. Could you play with my haih? //

BLANCHE. *(drinks)* (Needs more of a backbone) //

LILY. Tickle my arm.

(**BLANCHE** *demurs at first, but eventually does, she grazes* **LILY**'s *arm lightly with her fingernails. There's real longing.* **LILY** *starts looking through* **BLANCHE**'s *purse.*)

LILY. *You have mints?*

(**BLNCHE**. *I don't think so.*

LILY. *(pulls something out from her purse) Whassis?*

BLANCHE. *A pad Don't look through my stuff.*

(**LILY** *pulls out a gun and sits up, alarmed.*)

LILY. *What's that?*

BLANCHE. *Gimme that.*

(**BLANCHE** *grabs the gun away from* **LILY**.)

BLANCHE. *Girl's gotta protect herself.*

(**BLANCHE** *shoves the gun back in her purse, moves the purse away from* **LILY**. **LILY** *settles back into* **BLANCHE**'s *lap.*)

LILY. *I'm drunk. I want a mint-h!*

(**BLANCHE** *goes back to grazing* **LILY**'s *arm.*)

(*relaxing a bit*) I want a mint.

(**BLANCHE** *looks at her, strokes her arm. It's love.*)

BLANCHE. So were you in love at first sight?

LILY. With who?

BLANCHE. Hubby.

LILY. I was twelve. He used to buy me gum.

BLANCHE. Didn't the age difference bother your parents?

LILY. My father is much older than my mother.

BLANCHE. Where'd you meet?

LILY. My cousin's wedding, Julie, she drives a mitsubishi galant.

BLANCHE. That's nice.

LILY. (I like jaguars) //

BLANCHE. *(a bit of self-torture)* And you started dating? //

LILY. He took me for ice cream.

BLANCHE. *(curled irony)* And did you get all *excited* when you'd see him?

LILY. Aduknow.

BLANCHE. *(playful mocking)* Did you think, like, "*Oooh Prailines & Cream!*"?

LILY. *(scrunched face)* It was more I was nervous; my stomach hurt. I think I was excited, I was pretty young. I'm more matured now. Then I was a baby. Sometimes I would feel sick.

BLANCHE. A good sick?

LILY. *(guileless, a bit more drunk)* Well I'd throw up. But I'm more matured now; I don't throw up anymore; I got a lot of stomach viruses; my mother told me I had a sensitive stomach.

BLANCHE. and how did he propose?

*(**LILY** is lost in thought. There's a shift into melancholy.)*

BLANCHE. How did he propose // to

LILY. But I don't think it's right when people trick people.

BLANCHE. You // what –

LILY. I don't like that It's not right.

BLANCHE. Who tricked you?

LILY. *(drunk)* NO I didn't say that, you don't listen. What I said was I don't think it's RIGHT to trick someone.

*(**BLANCHE** backs off. She takes a sip of wine.)*

LILY. When did you first…have…like…sex…or whatever

BLANCHE. *(lying)* I can't remember.

LILY. How could you not remember. How old // were

BLANCHE. *I can't remember.*

   [STOP]

LILY. *Did. Did people tell you…what it was?*

BLANCHE. *(a dark undercurrent)* I kinda happened upon it.

(pause)

LILY. I thought it was if you touched someone a certain way. Or. If someone *touched* you? *(pause)* I was ignorant.

(**BLANCHE** *looks at her.*)

BLANCHE. No one talked about it to you?

LILY. And he said I wasn't a *virgin* anymore? So then I said that I would marry him. Because...my reputation would be ruined.

(pause)

(tearing up) But then I *was* a virgin ...

(long pause)

BLANCHE. *and you never told anyone?*

LILY. *My reputation // would be*

BLANCHE. *(tensing up)* So you just sit back and let him do it to you You just gonna sit back

[STOP]

LILY. I //

BLANCHE. *(taut, tough)* You're a VICTIM Zatwhatcha wanna be?

LILY. I'm not a // victim

BLANCHE. *(gritting her teeth, steely)* You got choices Make em. Every choice comes with a price Make the wrong one you pay up just the same.

Can't rely on *nobody* Just do it on your own. *[STOP]* Turn yourself inside out if that's what it takes Don't matter JUST FIX IT! *[STOP]* Be whoever you *need* to be Understand? You // understand me?

(**LILY** *shudders, jerks her head to the left, sharp intake of breath – it's the "ghost."*)

LILY. It's here –

BLANCHE. What?

LILY. *(panic) That –* its – It's in here That *–ghost* I – I just saw it again.

BLANCHE. Where?

*(**LILY** is still, alert; her eyes dart nervously. **BLANCHE** looks at **LILY**, gets increasingly spooked. She looks out, sensing a presence in the room. Her breathing gets unsteady. The silence is fraught with terror; they're both too frightened to move. It goes on like this for a bit.)*

*(**LILY** tentatively relaxes her posture a little bit.)*

LILY. I...I think it's gone now.

*(She approaches **BLANCHE** from behind, touches her lightly on the shoulder; **BLANCHE** gasps, shudders, jerks her head.)*

It's only me.

*(**BLANCHE** turns to see her.)*

BLANCHE. *(denial)* I don't believe in ghosts. *(She turns away from her; ineptly tries to make light of it.)* You givin' me the creeps.

LILY. *(hurt)* But...I...I saw it.

(beat)

BLANCHE. *(feigned indifference)* They can't haunt you if you don't acknowledge em Just pretend it's not there.

*(**LILY** looks at her, not quite comforted by this.)*

LILY. Will you sleep with me tonight?

*(**BLANCHE** hesitates. Eventually she nods yes.)*

We can sleep here in your room. I don't like to be alone.

BLANCHE. *(throws her a T-shirt)* Sleep in this.

*(They get dressed for bed. **LILY**'s having some trouble with the T-shirt.)*

LILY. I don't like it when you yell at me.

BLANCHE. I didn't yell at you.

LILY. *(drunk)* you did, you said "I'M AT THE BOTTOM OF THA EARTH I'M BLACK"

BLANCHE. (Sorry)

LILY. I don't like that I get scahed.

BLANCHE., I'm just worried about stuff; it's not you. I have a lot of. Uh – things on my mind.

LILY. *(a caper)* Like what-h? maybe I could help!

BLANCHE. *(lying)* My. My – loans and stuff are due.

LILY. from college?

BLANCHE. I used *up* my deferments they said. They're comin afer me.

LILY. But we're paying you

BLANCHE. yeah enough for food & c'est tout. *(bright)* I'll be ok – I'm just

LILY. You'll pay them back.

BLANCHE. *(forcing a smile)* I'll get a teachin job soon enough.

(pause)

LILY. Well. I have this checkbook – why don't I write you one.

BLANCHE. One what?

LILY. *Check* dibeh!

(beat)

BLANCHE. *No.*

LILY. I *want* to.

BLANCHE. It's not your responsibility.

LILY. *(sincere, lovingly)* You're my responsibility.

(long pause)

BLANCHE. *(moved, despite herself)* You don't even *know* me.

LILY. He said I should write you checks, how much is it for?

(LILY opens her purse and pulls out her checkbook.)

BLANCHE. You're crazy, I'm not taking *money* from you!

LILY. You helped me; now let me help you.

(BLANCHE looks at her.)

(LILY fills out and signs a check.)

(girlish) Look Don't I forge his signature good?

(LILY hands the check to her. BLANCHE looks at it. Slowly she takes it, looks down at it. It's real. She laughs. She looks at LILY and shakes her head. She looks down at the check again. She begins to weep – the tears come from a deep, deep, wounded place.)

BLANCHE. That's eight thousand dollars.

LILY. *(bright)* Now you can stay!

BLANCHE. I can't take this from you!

LILY. Yes you can.

(pause)

BLANCHE. *(embarrassed laughter)* Gracias Lily.

LILY. *De nada. (You're welcome.)*

BLANCHE. *Ojalá no se enoje. (I hope he doesn't get mad.)*

LILY. *El no se enterará. (He won't find out.)*

BLANCHE. *(laughs)* I hope you're right.

(LILY kisses BLANCHE on the cheek, a quick peck. LILY fluffs a pillow. BLANCHE gets under the covers.)

LILY. Let's go to bed I got a tennis lesson in the morning –

BLANCHE. I got laundry.

(snap blackout)

2.

(**BLANCHE**, **IKE** *and* **LILY**)

(*Five days later, morning. The living room.*)

(**BLANCHE** *is repainting the minimalist walls.* **IKE**'s *back from China, doing the crossword. He's wearing a suit; he looks especially groomed. He is wound up and angry.*)

(**LILY** *enters, she's on cloud nine, a woman in love.*)

LILY. I finished unpacking your stuff.

IKE. What?

LILY. Welcome back!

(**IKE** *continues with his crossword, not looking at her.* **LILY** *looks at him, cheery.*)

IKE. *Stop looking at me.*

LILY. What?

IKE. *(not looking up)* You keep lookin at me funny.

LILY. You look nice. You never wear suits to work.

IKE. *(weirdly uncomfortable)* I got a meeting.

LILY. With Jo?

(*beat*)

IKE. I gotta meet with some people.

(*beat*)

LILY. So how was it? did you see the wall?

IKE. That's Germany //

LILY. *Yeah* and also CHINA.

(*beat*)

LILY. I like that suit // on you

IKE. *(fillip of hostility)* WILL YOU SHUT UP ABOUT MY SUIT, I CAN WEAR A SUIT IF I WANNA WEAR A SUIT!

(**LILY** *looks at him, smiling indifferently.*)

LILY. *(irony)* Sexy when you get mad.

(**IKE** *knows he's insulted her but can't figure out how.* **BLANCHE** *smiles to herself and continues to paint.* **LILY** *picks up a book. Barthes's S/Z. She reads.*)

IKE. Hear any news? //

LILY. *(terse, not looking up)* I'm not pregnant.

(beat)

IKE. You spoke to the // doctor?

LILY. *(perfunctory)* There's nothing *wrong* with me //

IKE. Well there's nothing wrong with *me.*

(She reads. **IKE** *glowers at her.)*

IKE. *Did you hear what I said //*

LILY. "There's nothing wrong with me"

IKE. *(turns to face her)* Where were you last night?

LILY. Here.

IKE. I woke up you were gone.

LILY. I couldn't sleep.

BLANCHE. *(repainting, cheery)* We're running outta "snowball."

LILY. *(gets up to exit)* I'll get more.

IKE. Let the G get it.

(A little flirtatious pantomime behind Ike's back.)

(**LILY** *winks seductively at* **BLANCHE.**)

(**BLANCHE** *smiles flirtatiously and licks her lips.*)

(**IKE,** *sensing something, turns his head;* **BLANCHE** *instantly resumes her default painting position;* **LILY** *tries to act casual.*)

LILY. What –

IKE. Why don't you –

(**IKE** *cuts off mid-sentence. They resume flirting. He quickly shift back around, eyeballs them.*)

LILY. *(caught)* I'm not doing anything –

IKE. *What was that?*

LILY. *(innocently) What?*

> (**IKE** *slowly pivots back and resumes the crossword.* **BLANCHE** *giggles to herself.* **LILY** *pretends to be interested in* **IKE.***)*

> (**BLANCHE** *flashes her tit as* **LILY** *exits.* **LILY** *tries to stifle her laughter.)*

> (**IKE,** *sensing something, shifts abruptly to look at her and* **BLANCHE** *– who narrowly escapes exposure. He's getting angry.)*

IKE. *(punishing her)* Get me cream.

BLANCHE. It's on the table.

IKE. It's not on the table.

> (**BLANCHE** *walks over and takes the cream, which is three inches away from him, and positions it two inches from him – then flashes her best "innocent helper" smile. She goes back to painting.)*

> (**IKE** *gets up to feed the goldfish.)*

> *(to Kitty)* Hiiiiiiiiiiiiiiieeeeeeeeee. Hiiii honey!! Awwwwwwwwwww.

> (**BLANCHE** *looks over at him. She rolls her eyes. He senses her looking at him and quickly jerks his head to catch her. She deftly resumes painting. He sidles over to her. He leans against the wall, almost hovering.* **BLANCHE** *continues to paint.)*

Nice bracelets.

BLANCHE. What, oh these Oh they're bangles.

IKE. Very sharp, where'd you get em?

BLANCHE. *(lying)* The mall.

> *(She continues to paint.)*

IKE. *(to* **BLANCHE***)* You didn't by any chance mention anything to anyone did you?

BLANCHE. Bout what?

IKE. When you were in my office…? you didn't happen to
see anything?

BLANCHE. When I was cleaning?

IKE. Mention anything?

[STOP]

You wouldn't screw me would you?

*(**BLANCHE** looks him up and down.)*

BLANCHE. *(dryly)* I wouldn't.

IKE. Did you open your big mouth?

*(**BLANCHE** notices that half of his suit is now painted
white.)*

You look nervous.

BLANCHE. I. Your suit –

IKE. *(facetious)* What I don't MATCH?

BLANCHE. No – you –

*(**IKE** realizes he has paint on his suit.)*

*(**LILY** enters holding a paint can.)*

LILY. I can't find the – (HEEE.)

IKE. *(points at **BLANCHE**)* Why does she have to do that?

LILY. *(recites dutifully)* It's minimalism.

IKE. You think it's funny?

LILY. The decorator // said

IKE. *(upset)* IT'S NOT FUNNY.

LILY. I don't think it's funny!

*(**IKE** exits.)*

(calls after him) I-don't-think-it's –

*(She and **BLANCHE** lock eyes. They laugh and laugh
mischievously, but there's real intimacy.)*

*(The laughing grows uncontrollable, hysterical. Eventu-
ally it is drowned out by the sound of a woman speaking
French – a language lesson CD.)*

3.

(**LILY** *and* **IKE**)

(*Bedroom, night*)

(**IKE** *is going over receipts,* **LILY** *is practicing French. The CD overlaps their conversation.*)

TAPE. I am hungry. "J'ai faim."

LILY. "J'ai faim."

TAPE. I am thirsty. "J'ai soif."

LILY. "J'ai soif."

TAPE. I am frightened. "J'ai peur."

IKE. I'm missing // money.

LILY. "J'ai peur."

TAPE. I am cold. "J'ai fois."

LILY. "J'ai" //

IKE. I'm *missing money.*

TAPE. I am hot. "J'ai chaud."

> (*beat*)

LILY. From where?

IKE. The *bank.*

LILY. You gave // me a checkbook.

TAPE. I am afraid to take the plane. "J'ai peur de prendre l'avion."

IKE. You spent eight *grand* in one shot?

LILY. "J'ai peur de prendre l'avion."

> (**IKE** *slams the cd off.*)

IKE. Whaddayou spending eightthousandollars for.

> (*pause*)

LILY. I needed it.

IKE. For what

LILY. I don't have to tell you.

IKE. THAT'S MY MONEY

(short pause)

LILY. What's yours is mine Right? Isn't that what a marriage is? I take what I want from you and you take what you want // from me.

IKE. Why are you acting this way.

LILY. Because you're a liar.

IKE. How am I a liar?

(She turns to him.)

LILY. Because I talked to my sister and she told me you stole money from Jo and that they fired you last week. And that's why you're wearing a suit and screaming at me because you keep lying to me. Because you can't bribe me with money because we don't have any money. And no one's gonna hire you because everyone knows you're a thief.

(pause)

IKE. That's bullshit.

LILY. You *knew* she'd tell me.

(beat)

IKE. I didn't steal money. I. I re-allocated it.

LILY. Yeah.

(She turns the CD on again, he slams it right off.)

IKE. And don't you fucking tell me off. I won't be spoken to by my own wife like this and Im – HEY. *(grabs her)* I'm having a rough week, I don't need to come home you calling me names.

(silence)

And there are plenny a people who'd kill to work with me so shut your mouth You don't know what you're talking about. You hear me? I know how to run a business That's why you live good because I know what I'm doin.

LILY. Like your father, like how he ran a business?

IKE. Don't talk about my father.

LILY. *My sister said*

IKE. *You're sister's a fucking liar, alright?*

LILY. *No YOU'RE a liar. YOU.*

(*pause*)

(*quiet and so sad*) You tricked me…

[STOP]

(*He kisses her hair. She's momentarily helpless – he's got power over her.*)

IKE. I'm gonna take care of you.

LILY. Stop it //

IKE. I'm gonna take care of you…daddy's gonna take care of his baby ok?

(**LILY**, *in a single gesture, disentangles herself. She opens a drawer and grabs a bottle of expensive wine.*)

IKE. What's that?

(*She grabs a corkscrew and opens it expertly.*)

LILY. keeps the cork intact //

IKE. You don't *drink* //

LILY. I do now, *pouilly-fumé*, medium-bodied white //

IKE. Since when do you drink?

LILY. I started a wine cellar.

IKE. IN YOUR DRAW? //

LILY. Anna Maria taught me about *tasting* //

IKE. *Who?!* //

LILY. (*squinting*) She's an oenophile.

(*She swishes; slurps some wine. He looks at her.*)

IKE. *I don't want you drinking wine* //

LILY. (*swirling*) Honey, canteloupe //

IKE. You're not old enough // to

LILY. Oh I'm not *old* enough? *Really?* Talk more about that.

(*long pause*)

LILY. I think we should. Get an annulment.

IKE. What?

(pause)

(She turns, looks right at him.)

IKE. *(terrified)* Who's putting ideas in your head?

LILY. I have my *own* ideas.

IKE. Is it that nigger?

(She looks at him, enraged.)

[STOP]

IKE. Where's my money?

LILY. You are an ignorant. Old. Man //

(IKE *grabs the glass of wine as she's about to drink it and throws it in her face.)*

(leaning in) and you're turning into a spoiled little *brat* I don't like it.

(He does pushups. She's brewing.)

IKE. Fifteen. Sixteen.

(She starts attacking him, hitting him. It barely affects him. She kicks him, etc., but she's slight. He waits until she's out of breath. She's miserable, frustrated, humiliated, angry. He's impassive and his impassivity makes her angrier.)

Seventeen. *Don't do that again.*

(pause)

Eighteen. Nineteen. Twenty (I'm warning you)

(LILY *attacks him.* **BLANCHE** *enters with the laundry.)*

BLANCHE. *(smiling obliviously)* I forgot the whites. //

(IKE *bolts up.)*

IKE. WHADAISAY?

(LILY *eyeballs him; quiet and confident.)*

LILY. You don't have power over me.

[STOP]

(He smacks her across the face.)

(She smacks him right back.)

[STOP]

(In a single move, he punches **LILY** *square in the face.* **BLANCHE** *is terrified, paralyzed.)*

(In the next section they speak quickly over each other, it's a bit chaotic.)

IKE. Do NOT touch my person do you hear me, you don't EVER touch me, EVER, do you hear // me

BLANCHE. I //

IKE. And YOU you just bought a ticket to your own funeral did you // hear me.

LILY. *(cups her hand over her eye)* You // hit me

IKE. *(to* **BLANCHE***)* You're DEAD, did // you hear me.

BLANCHE. Who // me

LILY. *¿Me lastimó, // viste lo que hizo?*

BLANCHE. *¿Estás // bien?*

IKE. WHAT DID // YOU SAY TO HER?

LILY. *Tengo que irme de aquí; promete que nos iremos.*

BLANCHE. I promise //

IKE. WHAT DID // SHE SAY TO YOU??

LILY. *(still stunned)* You hit // me.

IKE. *(Shame. Then to* **BLANCHE***)* Good-bye, back in your // cage

BLANCHE. I //

LILY. (You // hit me.)

IKE. Get // out!

BLANCHE. Lily //

IKE. GEEET OOOOUTTT!!

(snap blackout)

4.

(Sounds of tennis balls being lobbed about.)

(The lounge area of an indoor tennis court.)

(LILY *and* **SHELLY** *in tennis outfits, headbands, sweaty.*
LILY *is twirling her racquet.)*

(She has a black eye.)

SHELLY. The silks were nice. We saw a silkworm farm. A
place where they make silkworms. *(beat)* I mean not
silkworms I mean, HA HA, where the silkworms are.
Where they *make silk. (beat)* I was gagging from the
smell. ERT.

LILY. Does it smell?

SHELLY. (The silk is nice but-h.)

LILY. My backhand's improving Gerard said.

SHELLY. My knee hurts.

(A pause as **LILY** *adjusts a string on her racquet.)*

LILY. So, how are you feeling?

SHELLY. When I was carrying Ricky I was bad, when I had
Joey – Stevie – but // aduknow

LILY. Do you want something else to drink?

SHELLY. I wish they had sprite; I don't like this OTHAH
CRAP-ah.

(beat)

LILY. Do you know anything about Chicago? //

SHELLY. Windy. //

LILY. You were never theh? //

SHELLY. *(picks up glass)* Wisconsin, Ohio, aduknow. *(sips)*
*You know who's theh – Oprah. (Sips, then pushes glass away
with histrionic disgust.)* ERT I'm NAUSHUS.
You want my lemon?

(pause)

(The sounds of tennis balls being lobbed.)

SHELLY. You need to be pregnant.

LILY. Yeah.

SHELLY. "Yeah."

(*beat*)

SHELLY. What's with you?

(*pause*)

LILY. I'm getting an annulment.

(**SHELLY** *laughs at her.*)

LILY. It's not funny.

SHELLY. (*dismissing*) Oh please. The string on my racquet broke look at this –

LILY. He stole money.

SHELLY. We'll get the money back.

LILY. (*after a beat*) He *lied.*

SHELLY. You're not getting an *annulment.*

LILY. I'm bisexual. I was talking to Blanche that's what she said.

(**LILY** *sucks on the lemon wedge innocuously.*)

SHELLY. What's what who said?

LILY. I'm not a lesbian.

SHELLY. Who's *Blanche?*

LILY. My maid.

SHELLY. Why is your *maid* telling you you're a bisexual?

(*pause*)

LILY. (*regretting telling her*) Tell me more about the silk farm.

SHELLY. Is your *maid* a bisexual?

LILY. (*sucking the lemon*) Lesbian.

SHELLY. *Back up* //

LILY. You want gum? //

SHELLY. NO I DON'T WANT GUM.

(*pause*)

LILY. I'm moving to Chicago.

SHELLY. *(laughing)* With who your *maid?*

LILY. She has tenure track

SHELLY. *(giddy) Op-*stay already I *caaan't.*

LILY. Northwestern. It's the ivy league.

[STOP]

(**SHELLY** *is speechless.*)

LILY. She has connections //

SHELLY. What is she gonna teach toilet scrubbing?

LILY. Semiotics //

SHELLY. Ok. *you're not a lesbian //*

LILY. Which is //

SHELLY. I-DON'T-WANT-TO-KNOW-WHAT-IT-IS.

LILY. She has a PhD.

SHELLY. Yeah she's a freakin genius.

LILY. She quotes poetry do you?

SHELLY. No I don't quote POETRY Lilian I'm too busy cleaning up my kids' VOMIT. *(pause)* I gotta go to my jeweler It's almost six –

LILY. Wait //

SHELLY. You smell. go shower.

LILY. *(very tender)* I love someone; I never had that before.

(**SHELLY** *scrutinizes her like meat.*)

SHELLY. *Shame on you.*

[STOP]

(*She gets up to leave.* **LILY** *grabs her arm.*)

LILY. Shel //

SHELLY. *I thought you wanted kids.*

(*beat*)

LILY. I'm on the pill.

SHELLY. You're *what?* I thought //

LILY. Don't tell him.

(*A recognition of* **LILY**'s *duplicity slowly registers on* **SHELLY**'s *face.*)

SHELLY. I have to go //

LILY. Please // don't

SHELLY. No I don't want to hear this *shit.*

LILY. *(heartbroken) Why?*

SHELLY. Why, because it's making me SICK. *(beat)* I'm *pregnant* and you're making me SICK.

LILY. I //

SHELLY. I was doing you a *favor.* You think JoJo wanted to go into business with your low-life husband – *that was from me! (beat)* And then you spit in my *face?*

LILY. I'm sorry.

SHELLY. *Pig.*

(pause)

LILY. I appreciate everything you // and

SHELLY. *(shaking her head; to herself)* No I don't *want* your appreciation Don't *waste it on me.*

(LILY zips up her tennis racquet in its case.)

LILY. I thought we could be...*close.* I

SHELLY. *(looks at her – steely)* You're. Committing. Suicide.

LILY. *(feigning bravery)* People can think what they want //

SHELLY. You're not a *fucking* lesbian //

LILY. *(quiet tears, but trying to stay composed)* I'm //

SHELLY. And we'll see how you don't care what people think, we'll see. And don't you DARE come crawling to me on your hands and knees because I'll kick you right in the throat. You'll get *nothing.*

LILY. *(stunned)* Don't talk to me like that.

SHELLY. How should I talk to you? What do you feel you *deserve?* you feel proud of yourself?

LILY. I – I thought I could come to you.

SHELLY. *Why?* You think you can bring your filthy news to me? Do you have such a *low* opinion of me?

(silence)

LILY. *(a plea)* But. I'm. I'm...not *happy.*

SHELLY. *So be unhappy.*

LILY. Like you?

SHELLY. That's right. Like me You're damn *right* like me –

(**LILY** *exits.*)

I feel sorry for your husband.

5.

(**BLANCHE** *and* **LILY**)

(*The living room, daytime*)

(**BLANCHE** *is dustbusting.* **LILY** *is eating candies and little confections and chatting excitedly.*)

LILY. And there were peonies and hydrangeas // and

BLANCHE. And were they just *petals?*

LILY. No.

BLANCHE. See?

(**BLANCHE** *gives her a peck on the cheek.*)

LILY. And I became a member of Channel 13!

(**LILY** *produces a tote/duffel bag with the PBS logo emblazoned.*)

BLANCHE. Nice //

LILY. (And-also-they-gave-me-a-comb) //

BLANCHE. Did you make your // flash cards?

LILY. And there was a flower shaped like – oh what's it called? *(snap, snap)* OOLIE.

BLANCHE. A forsythia?

LILY. No.

BLANCHE. A daisy?

LILY. A *hyacinth.*

BLANCHE. Oh "the hyacinth girl."

LILY. What? //

BLANCHE. What? Oh that's // from

LILY. Yeah a flower.

BLANCHE. Shaped like a hyacinth?

LILY. No.

BLANCHE. *(dustbusting under her feet)* (Lift.)

LILY. No it was – insects – it was like insects, like these. Uh. *Bright* insects, and they were green, and they would form themselves like that, it was very mysterious

BLANCHE. To escape predators.

LILY. YES.

BLANCHE. It's not mysterious it's nature survival of the species.

LILY. Oh.

   (beat)

BLANCHE. *(down)* How's your eye?

LILY. Better //

BLANCHE. Where's Rich?

LILY. What?

BLANCHE. I mean – hubby.

LILY. Aduknow he stays out late.

BLANCHE. He's watching me. I keep thinking he's gonna turn a corner and appear outta nowhere He's like a ghost. He scares me.

LILY. He thinks you got him fired.

BLANCHE. *(laughs, exasperated)* I was there *one* day.

LILY. Where?

BLANCHE. His *office*, I'm not *that* good at bookkeepin!

LILY. He's paranoid.

   (beat)

BLANCHE. You goin to your sister's?

   (LILY *doesn't respond, a shift.)*

LILY. I'm not talking to her.

BLANCHE. Why?

LILY. No reason.

BLANCHE. She loves you.

LILY. She doesn't like *you.*

BLANCHE. *(chipper)* Cause I'm black and she's racist it's perfectly consistent.

LILY. She said the n word.

BLANCHE. I heard, I don't mind. It's just a signifier – and what are signifiers? //

LILY. Arbitrary //

BLANCHE. And what is all language? //

LILY. Metaphor.//

BLANCHE. Because. //

LILY. There's no relationship between things and words //

BLANCHE. "Necessary" //

LILY. (Necessary) but you keep telling me that she *doesn't* love me.

BLANCHE. Well – her love is *degraded* but she has good intentions.

> *(beat)*

LILY. She said I was a pig.

BLANCHE. Why would she say that?

> *(pause)*
>
> Did you quarrel?
>
> *(beat)*

LILY. I told her.

BLANCHE. Told her what?

> *(beat)*
>
> *(senses something)* Told her what.
>
> **(BLANCHE** *freezes.)*
>
> Why would you do that.
>
> *(beat)*

LILY. I wanted to prepare her.

BLANCHE. For.

LILY. When we go //

BLANCHE. *Go?* //

LILY. To *Chicago.*

> *(beat)*

BLANCHE. *(faint exasperation)* I don't have that job yet darling.

LILY. You said it was a cinch

BLANCHE. *(smile evaporates)* Aint nuthin a cinch in this world din I teach you that? *(beat)* and your sister's got a big mouth –

LILY. Call Bell.

BLANCHE. *(to herself) (I'm-gonna-get-fired-O // -my-god.)*

LILY. *Y a tí que te importa nos vamos para Chicago.*

BLANCHE. Yeah Chicago but he could gimme the boot to morrow //

LILY. He won't do // that

BLANCHE. And-he HITS!

LILY. Just once –

BLANCHE. *(attacks with fevered urgency)* No – you don't hit women I'm sorry. Look at you. Do you like how you look? // Do you

LILY. No. //

BLANCHE. like making yourself a *victim* because you *put* yourself here. This is what you chose to make a your life Not me.

(a pause)

*(***BLANCHE*** withdraws from* **LILY***.)*

*(***LILY*** turns to her, worried. She tentatively goes to* **BLANCHE***.)*

LILY. *(deep, profound tenderness)* I won't let anything happen to you.

*(***BLANCHE*** slowly turns to* **LILY***; those eyes; it's heart-breaking.)*

(a short pause)

BLANCHE. *(toughness beginning to melt)* How you gonna protect me. You just a kid.

(short pause)

LILY. I will protect you.

*(***BLANCHE*** looks at* **LILY***.)*

(beat)

(She touches LILY's cheek. Softens.)

(pause)

(BLANCHE sees herself in Lily's eyes. It's mesmerizing. She smiles a faint smile, tinged with sadness.)

BLANCHE. *(undercurrent of deep worry)* Know how stupid I was at seventeen? That's when I left home…took me years before I figured out what I was doin with my life.

(beat)

LILY. *(sweetly encouraging)* and now you're almost there.

(BLANCHE snaps back into the moment.)

BLANCHE. I know that; I'm almost there I know.

(Again, a shift back into something very interior.)

(Her eyes fill with worry, her voice gets a bit higher here.)

BLANCHE. *(deep fear, almost a whisper)* But the world's a dangerous place.

LILY. I'm not scared!

(BLANCHE is faraway.)

BLANCHE. *(gently and not just pain, sorrow)* You say that but you don't know what it's like. *(beat)* You can be hurt and never…never recover. *(pause; then to herself)* think you can end it…but it doesn't!

LILY. Doesn't what?

BLANCHE. End! It doesn't just end, doesn't go away! I – I can't explain it to you…You…you can't understand…

LILY. But – you're telling me I have to make choices.

BLANCHE. *(snapping out of it)* But // not

LILY. You're saying don't be a victim – //

BLANCHE. *(a shift)* I'm. No – //

LILY. That's what you // said!

(BLANCHE turns on LILY quite suddenly. it's ferocious but she is very still, focused.)

BLANCHE. *(taut, tense)* No I'm sayin stay – stay and fight for something. You gotta take up the damn cudgels, not run away! *(beat)* You can walk out that door but you never really leave! You think you do – but you come back to the same thing again and again! You need to meet it head on!

(pause)

LILY. *(imploring, confused)* You promised me we'd leave.

(BLANCHE *looks at* **LILY** *– another shift, 180 degrees. Her heart melting, she's suddenly filled with guilt over her outburst.)*

BLANCHE. *(sorrow)* I know.

[STOP]

(BLANCHE *– in a single gesture – grabs* **LILY** *tight, holds her for dear life.)*

[STOP]

(BLANCHE *quickly, hungrily covers her with kisses, she's filled with need. Then – abruptly, she stops, looks at* **LILY,** *holding her shoulders.)*

(pain still seeping through, fearful) I know honey I know… but we gotta look at reality here.

LILY. You're the one not looking at reality!

BLANCHE. We can't just leave, sweetie.

LILY. *(desperate to convince her)* I have money saved up. We can live on that for a while.

BLANCHE. Then what?

LILY. I…I don't know.

BLANCHE. You don't know because you're living in a dream, that's why –

LILY. There's places in Wicker park…We could get books We could – *(beat)* You said I could be a whole other person…That's what you said.

(LILY *looks at her.* **BLANCHE** *cannot make eye contact with* **LILY** *over the next few lines.)*

BLANCHE. *(impossibly vulnerable)* I just can't…

LILY. What are you talking about? Of course you can.

(long pause)

BLANCHE. *(almost in tears, very tiny)* I c-can't – I can't – make myself into what I – w-what you need me to be.

(Pause. **LILY** *looks at her, perplexed.)*

LILY. But…I don't want you to make yourself – into // anything I

*(***BLANCHE*** *abruptly turns to* **LILY,** *interrupting her, her demeanor suddenly cold.)*

BLANCHE. *(tightening; her voice drops)* That's-not-what-I-meant.

*(***LILY*** *stops for a moment, somewhat startled.)*

LILY. What did you mean?

(beat)

BLANCHE. I just. I think we should just leave it alone. It's – this – is - it isn't realistic.

LILY. I know you'll get that job.

BLANCHE. *(snaps abruptly)* How? How can you know I haven't even sent my goddam resume yet.

LILY. You're *smart.* I never met anyone // as smart as you

BLANCHE. *(incapable of restraining her rage, vicious) Because you have no life experience.* Are you *joking? (pause)* You *child. (Beat. She grabs her face.)* Look at me. I'm forty-fucking-three years old I'm cleaning *houses* on my hands // and knees

LILY. But you're working // on

BLANCHE. *No! NO I can't work anymore! I'm at the end of it, do you understand? I can't live anymore* I'm *tired!*

LILY. But //

BLANCHE. *(a quick explosion)* I'M-TIRED!

(A deafening silence. They both stand, frozen.)

LILY. *(quiet humiliation)* I'm … trying to have more… life experiences.

(pause)

BLANCHE. I know.

(pause)

LILY. *(weakly)* Don't call me a child.

[STOP]

*(We see a smile spread slowly across **BLANCHE**'s face. Her countenance changes completely. They're saved.)*

BLANCHE. It's fine.

We don't gotta make a deal out of it.

(bright) As Bubbles Sills used to say. Leave the drama on the stage.

*(**LILY** looks at her.)*

(forced smile, girlishness) We just have to call your sister, tell her it was a joke, kay?

LILY. She won't believe that.

BLANCHE. Say it was a gag //

LILY. But –

BLANCHE. Say it was a // gag then kissy kiss make

LILY. No.

BLANCHE. up & drop the whole // thing.

LILY. She won't believe that //

BLANCHE. *(strained sweetness, smile)* Just call her.

LILY. I //

BLANCHE. *(spasm of rage)* CALL HER!

(long pause)

*(**BLANCHE** stands there, closes her eyes; she's exhausted. It's as if her entire history has finally caught up with her here. She grasps on to a piece of furniture, to stablize herself.)*

LILY. *(sweet, sad)* I don't want to drop the whole thing.

[STOP]

BLANCHE. We can't do this.

LILY. *(tearful, crushed)* We can

BLANCHE. No. We can't.

LILY. *(soft)* Why?

> *(pause)*
>
> *(paralyzed with grief and confusion) So what was* what was this? You were telling me things. why? because I'm – *gullible?*

BLANCHE. That // ain't it.

LILY. Taking my money? // You knew I'd

BLANCHE. This is not a sustainable *relationship.*

LILY. *(hurt)* WHY?

BLANCHE. *(passionately)* Because I want you to be HAPPY and you WONT with ME.

LILY. I WILL.

BLANCHE. You're saying that cause you'll grasp onto anything. I was you once, I know – You haven't found yourself.

LILY. I HAVE.

BLANCHE. *(shutting her down)* NO. You HAVEN'T. And you won't *ever* with me, *ever.*

> **(LILY** *is lost, in disbelief. A long unbroken silence.)*

LILY. I. I just told my *sister.*

> *(beat)*

BLANCHE. Call her and tell her you // were

LILY. SHE WON'T BELIEVE THAT!

> [STOP]

BLANCHE. She will. She will – just –

> **(LILY** *gets her coat, etc.)*

BLANCHE. Where are you going? //

LILY. I don't know.

BLANCHE. *(increasing panic)* Sweetie – don't – don't leave. Let's – we can figure something out.

LILY. *(weakly, barely able to speak)* Why.

BLANCHE. *(urgent, grasping for words)* Let me – Let me help you.

LILY. You want to "help me."

"I help you...and you help me."

*(In an instant **LILY** jumps to the conclusion that she's unearthed the whole horrible truth about this relationship. Something's dying in her.)*

(Pause. The whole thing slows down.)

LILY. *(weakly, quiet)* Could I get my money back.

*(**BLANCHE** looks at her, startled. A pause.)*

BLANCHE. *(fearful)* What?

LILY. The money I gave you. I need it back.

BLANCHE. *(grasping)* I can't – I can't get that I already used it.

LILY. For what.

BLANCHE. *(panicked)* You know that – I used it, I paid my loans.

(pause)

You gave me a check

*(**LILY** slowly lifts her head to meet **BLANCHE**'s gaze.)*

(long silence)

(then, finally:)

LILY. *(quiet, through tears)* You are *so. Dead.*

*(**BLANCHE** looks at her, terrified, stunned. A pause.)*

BLANCHE. *(fear)* What are you talkin about? You gave me a *check.*

*(Pause. **LILY** slowly turns away from **BLANCHE**. She's palpably alone.)*

LILY. *(completely helpless)* You're *tricking* me.

*(**LILY**, in a daze, tries to gather her things..)*

BLANCHE. *(frenetic)* Wait //

LILY. *(vulnerable)* You're *tricking* me I // know you are

BLANCHE. (desperate, pleading) Lily come on –

(**LILY** *storms out.*)

(**BLANCHE** *just stands there, very still.*)

(long, long silence)

(**BLANCHE** *dazedly looks around the room, tries to orient herself. She sees a rag, picks it up, trying to snap out of it.)*

(She looks for the caddy, sees it, walks to it, picks up the windex, still unsteady.)

(She walks to a mirror, sprays the windex, wipes it with a rag.)

(As she is wiping, she catches her reflection in the mirror. She is transfixed by her own image.)

(She stretches out her arm as if holding a gun.)

(She sprays the windex, watches the liquid drip down, waits a moment.)

(She sprays again, waits another moment.)

(Sprays again.)

(Again. Again, again, faster and faster as the liquid drips down the mirror and her face becomes a blur.)

6.

(**LILY, SHELLY** *and* **CLAUDINE**)

(A diner. Muzak is playing lightly in the background. We hear the muffled voices of other diners, clanking silverware.)

*(**LILY** is sitting alone at a booth. She is miserable. She wears sunglasses and a fur coat.)*

*(**SHELLY** enters with **CLAUDINE**. She's wearing a "Chairman Mao" suit she purchased in China.)*

(a pause)

SHELLY. *(brusque)* What.

(pause)

I'm here, what.

LILY. I...

[STOP]

SHELLY. WHAT.

LILY. I. I just.

*(**LILY** takes off her sunglasses. Her eyes are completely red, tears are streaming down her face. Her voice sounds oddly high; she speaks from the back of her throat, very frail.)*

SHELLY. You what?

LILY. I stopped taking *(pause)* I –
SHELLY. WHAT.

(She's crying and can't get the words out.)

LILY. I stopped taking...my...
SHELLY. You what?
LILY. My...
SHELLY. I can't hear what you're saying.
LILY. I // s-s-sstopped
SHELLY. Ok, look I'm gonna // go
LILY. My PILL.

(beat)

LILY. I stopped taking…my…my pill I. I stopped – I stopped taking my *pill* I…

(**LILY** *attempts a hopeful smile, even a conspiratorial giggle.*)

(**SHELLY** *just looks at her.*)

(**LILY** *earnestly takes* **SHELLY**'s *hand.*)

(**SHELLY** *just stands there.*)

(trying, to no avail, to be conversational) I…I…

(**LILY** *releases quiet, helpless sobs. She looks down ashamed.* **SHELLY** *stands, observing: neither cruel nor compassionate, but almost anthropologic, as if this is a new, unfamiliar, alien specimen.*)

(**LILY** *weakly releases* **SHELLY**'s *hand. It drops back to her side.*)

(The lights dim very slowly on **LILY**'s *sobbing.*)

End Act Two

ACT THREE
Para los Muertos

1.

(Living room. The vase of dead chrysanthemums is replaced by fresh flowers, bright green in color, and supplemented with a few other vases, also of brightly colored flowers. **BLANCHE** *is listening to music.)*

*(***IKE*** *enters. She senses someone – turns, thinking it's* **LILY**. *It's him. He picks up the remote; turns off the radio.)*

IKE. Whatcha doin?

BLANCHE. I was listening to that.

IKE. Chillin? *(snaps his fingers)* Chillin out? *(snaps his fingers)*

BLANCHE. I'm taking a *break.* I'm legally entitled // to

IKE. Legally //

BLANCHE. breaks, yeah, that's right you're legally entitled to things.

IKE. Are you interested in the Law Anna Marie?

BLANCHE. The name's Blanche.

IKE. Ya know My dad loved the Law. *True. (pause)* He was a very great man.

BLANCHE. (Want somm to // drink?)

IKE. *(produces a picture of him)* He's my spittin image.

(shows her)

IKE. That's a derby hat, from the old times, check that out. he was a sharp dresser wasn't he? he used to work in textiles. He built himself from the ground up and then they wrecked him. They pillaged him, they stole the rug out from under him He died with nothing; and he had greatness in him. (*Beat. Saccharine smile*) But that's how people are. Wouldn't you agree?

BLANCHE. uh huh.

(*She smiles a strained smile, looks away. He puts the photograph back in his wallet.*)

IKE. I get the sense you don't like me.

(*He walks to the fishbowl.*)

(**IKE** *feeds Kitty.*)

IKE. *Kitty* likes me.. (*to Kitty*) Hiiiiiiiiiieeeeeeeeeeee.

(**BLANCHE** *anxiously watches him feed Kitty.*)

BLANCHE. (*attempting to finesse it*) Kitty likes the new algae I can tell.

IKE. Look at that look That's love.

BLANCHE (*trying to impress him, nervous*) You know actually goldfish *can't* love. Neuronally speaking I mean They aren't wired for it.

(**IKE** *turns his head, slowly. Eyeballs her.*)

IKE. (*quiet, coiled*) Do-you-what-love-is?

(*A beat, as* **BLANCHE** *tries to finesse it.*)

BLANCHE. (*plastering on a smile*) It's – so // subjective

IKE. (*explosion*) SO-DON'T-SPEAK-FA-FISH!

(**BLANCHE** *holds the smile, rather tensely, slowly swivels back.*)

[STOP]

BLANCHE. I // think

IKE. Why don't you go out on dates?

(*beat*)

BLANCHE. Pardon?

IKE. *Dates?* With *boys?*

(*beat*)

BLANCHE. I don't know that that's relevant to my job.

(He scrutinizes her; she feels him watching her but won't look at him. She thumbs awkwardly through a magazine.)

IKE. You won't look me in the eye; why's that?

(She turns to him.)

BLANCHE. look you // in

IKE. You look my wife in the eye Why's that.

[STOP]

BLANCHE. I'm sorry?

(beat)

IKE. Are you? //

BLANCHE. What? //

IKE. Sorry?

[STOP]

BLANCHE. *(laughs)* Ok, this is slightly – uh

IKE. *(shift, more intense)* See these *rivets?*
On these jeans?
These are like *eyes.*
My eyes are *rivets.* I have eyes all over my *person.*
I can see everything...
there isn't a THING you can hide from me.

BLANCHE. *(tense smile)* uh. I don't know what you mean.

(pause)

IKE. So you a *college* girl, huh?

BLANCHE. That's right.

*(**IKE** looks at her, smiles.)*

IKE. Nope!

BLANCHE. What?

IKE. Neva went to college.

(Beat. She smiles brightly, heightening the performance.)

BLANCHE. *(glib)* uhh. I went to princeton then brown Got a PhD //

IKE. *(plainly)* Don't waste my time, arite? I had you checked out.

(beat)

BLANCHE. *(laughs)* Um. I think *you* a little checked out, cuz this is kinda over tha top.

IKE. Why you cleanin my toilets you got a Ph fuckin D huh?

BLANCHE. *(rolling her eyes)* I wuz in Paris a bunch a years; I'm not acclimatized // to

IKE. *(makes inverted quotation marks with his fingers, hard sarcasm)* Oh not // "acclimatized"

BLANCHE. I reject // establishment –

IKE. *(laughing)* You know you act like you're so much better than me You're not even *educated*!

BLANCHE.. I speak four languages //

IKE. *(unfettered exasperation)* YEAH! *BULLSHIT*-&-THREE-OTHAHS!

[STOP]

*(***BLANCHE*** *artifices a Cheshire cat smile. A shift here.)*

BLANCHE. Sounds like you a little jealous a me huh?

*(***IKE*** *laughs softly.)*

IKE. *(sarcasm)* Well… now that you mention it I actually always *dreamed* a bein a career criminal // so

BLANCHE. *(plainly)* But you *are* a criminal.

[STOP]

IKE. *(staccato, quiet)* (You got a big mouth You know that)

BLANCHE. *(shakes her head no)* Ain't my fault. Tried to make yrself inta sumthin and ya failed. It happens.

*(***IKE*** *chortles to himself.)*

IKE. *(tries to make a joke out of it)* I'm a failure?

BLANCHE. *(a shift from caustic to a bit more plaintive)* You thought you could be anything you wanted dintcha. Tried to make yourself a whole other person. Kicked screamed all you wanted Din matter It's the *system.* *(to*

herself) You don't got a choice in it. Don't matter what you do Gonna crush you anyhow. *(pause; still interior)* It's a history a failure ain't it; ya whole life.

(IKE looks at her – this all resonates uncannily with him. It freaks him out – he pushes back whatever fear she draws out of him.)

IKE. *(bravado, smiling)* I'm a failure? Yr funny. I made 200 grand in one year. NET! You think you'll ever see money like that? You're a joke. Look at this HOUSE –

BLANCHE. *(pointed, almost prescient)* This *house.* You know what this house is? A *casket.* A big *ugly* casket That's what you built. *(beat)* An' you'll die in it.

(His smile fades. Pause.)

IKE. *(pretends to be impervious)* What about you? How you gonna die Huh?

(beat; then steely) Bet I can guess.

(An impasse. She turns to leave, he stops her.)

IKE. Oh, and by the way? We *are* white; people of spanish descent are *caucasian,* I looked it up.

(She turns to him.)

BLANCHE. *(sarcasm)* Congratulations.

(She starts to exit.)

IKE. *(fake pleasantry)* Oh one more thing.

(She stops in her tracks.)

(doesn't turn to look at him)

BLANCHE. What's that.

IKE. *(coy)* How do I say this. Uh – do you know a guy named Richard Nesbitt?

*(On the words "Richard Nesbitt" **BLANCHE** becomes very still. Her breathing becomes unsteady. She doesn't look at him. **IKE** takes in her reaction. She slowly shuts her eyes, the cells in her body are dying, one at a time. Her composure begins to crack.)*

IKE. From philly? Rich Nesbitt? *(pause)* It's kinda sad actually. Couple months back his own daughter – Blanche? – she tried to shoot him. Coulda killed him. Didn't but she just left him there. He coulda died. Cops are lookin for her and it's kinna serious cuz if they find her she's off to jail. *(beat)* Know where she might be?

(He walks to her very very slowly, a spider trapping its prey.)

(gets very close to her) Why do you think she'd do sumthin like that huh?

(pause)

BLANCHE. *(deep sadness, almost a whisper)* Thought I could end it… *(to herself, a recognition)* but it don't end.

IKE. *(clueless)* End what?

(Long pause. A smile slowly spreads across his face; he's openly gloating.)

Guess you just got that criminal instinct, huh?

(Her expression changes. Her lips curl into a tiny, taut smile.)

(She turns to him.)

BLANCHE. Criminal instinct Yeah That must be it. *(smiles ironically)* Must be a relief fa you Huh? I make sense to you now? *(tiny laugh)* O I know what you thinking. Think I don't? Guess what. I built my whole LIFE around what you think a me ALL OF YOU! *(tiny smile again; then quick)* You-think-I-don't-see-it? Think-I-don't-bash-my-*head*-against-the-wall-seein-it-every-damn-day-a-my-*life*? *(STOP; the pain mounting here:)* That's why I made my own raw materials, *had* none Had to make somm up What else I *got*? No wallpaper on my walls *Flash cards…* Kant…Aristotle…

IKE. *(affectless)* Wow great story Maybe when you get to *prison* you can write ya memoirs – //

(He walks determinedly to the phone, picks up the receiver. She goes after him;)

BLANCHE. I ain't goin to prison. You can forget about calling the cops I ain't goin.

(She lunges impulsively – grabs the phone from him. She's shaking, panicked, not sure what's next.)

[STOP]

IKE. *(looking out, quiet but tense)* Gimme the phone.

*(**BLANCHE** just stands there, shaking, terrified, cornered. It's a complete impasse. An extremely tense silence.)*

BLANCHE. *(faking bravery, but it's hard)* She *loves* me

(A beat. He slowly turns to her, dumbfounded – it's true and he knows it, sees it in her. Just saying the words jolts her out of the moment, slowly transports her. A realization.)

(almost radiant) Don't matter what you do…cuz she loves *me.*

*(**BLANCHE** smiles softly. **IKE**'s humiliation starts to morph into a quiet, frightening rage.)*

[STOP]

*(**IKE** grabs **BLANCHE** by the hair. Hard. In a single gesture he jerks his arm to his side; she goes crashing down with it, screaming, dropping the phone. **IKE** drags **BLANCHE** over to the paint trough.)*

BLANCHE. *(terrified)* I'm – NO!!

(In one gesture he shoves her face in it. Hard. He holds her head down – suffocating her.)

(She tries to scratch his face, hit him, but he pins her hand down. He finally lifts her head up.)

NO! NO –

(He shoves her head back into the paint trough, pushing her face hard into the pan.)

*(After a long while **BLANCHE** stops struggling.)*

(He pulls her head out, releases her body.)

(She's coughing, spitting out paint, no energy, shaking, wiping white paint out of her eyes, her face, her hair.)

(**IKE** *slowly rises, facing a mirror. He's numb. He sees his reflection. Grows transfixed by his own image here – he's a stranger. Slowly the recognition builds, the guilt starts to surface, the awfulness.*)

(**BLANCHE** *starts to move. He turns to look at her.*)

(*He can't look at her.*)

IKE. *(gruff)* I live good.
(feeling welling up) I got a nice house.
(pushing back tears) I don't want nuthin from nobody.

(**BLANCHE** *looks, out, reaching for transcendence with all her might.*)

BLANCHE. *(a sad smile)* Candle in the window.

IKE. *(denial, anger, pushing off guilt:)* I don't hurt *nobody.*

BLANCHE. *(immersing herself in the beauty of her own vision)* House in Wicker Park.
Books homes trees.

(pause)

Stars in the sky.

(*The space has transformed. We're in* **BLANCHE**'s *room.*)

(**BLANCHE** *sits alone. It's dark except for a soft light.*)

2.

(We hear foosteps descending down a staircase into the basement. **BLANCHE** *hears it – She looks towards the door, wipes paint off her face. Sits up expectantly. She is working to push past the humiliation of the last scene, but it won't leave.)*

(LILY *opens the door to* **BLANCHE***'s room.)*

(A shaft of light illuminating the two of them.)

(LILY*'s hair is different – swept up.)*

(She tries to make herself impervious to Blanche's pain here but keeps being thrown off balance by the fierce longing and sadness welling up in her.)

BLANCHE. *(smiling expectantly)* I wuz hoping you'd find me.

(pause)

LILY. *(breathing unsteadily)* The decorator's coming tomorrow.

We're turning your room into a nursery.

(pause)

BLANCHE. You're. *(pause)* That's //

LILY. He'll be here at ten. Pack up.

BLANCHE. *(flicker of hope)* Wait – I –

LILY. We're not calling the police.

(Pause. **BLANCHE** *summons the courage to speak.)*

BLANCHE. *(with difficulty; comes from a wounded, raw place)* I *love* you.

(silence)

LILY. *(not looking at her)* You left this in my room.

(She tosses a book onto the bed.)

BLANCHE. *(painful admission)* I never been in love before… I'm forty three years old I never been in love wit *nobody.*

(We see **LILY** *look at her. Her heart is breaking. Slowly, we watch her work to stamp back the feeling.)*

LILY. Do you have my money.

(pause)

BLANCHE. I'll.

I'll get it for you I – here I got…some of it I

(She rushes to her wallet – holds up a wad of cash – extends her arm.)

(long pause)

(Pause. **LILY** starts to melt a bit. **BLANCHE** looks at her, hopeful.)

LILY. (tentative) What was the money for?

(beat)

BLANCHE. I…borrowed from the wrong people…they were threatening // me They

LILY. (snapping back) Do you know what you are?

(pause)

A good teacher.

I was lacking; I never learned any lessons.

(The emotion starts to build.)

Now I have

Life.

Experience.

[STOP]

BLANCHE. (quick) I'll get you the rest a the money I // just

LILY. (quiet, raw pain, looks down, fists clenched) I-don't-give-a-shit-about-the-money.

[STOP]

(**LILY** composes herself; stands erect, like a statue.)

BLANCHE. (speaks quickly) I'll tell you anything you wanna know – ask me – anything…

(beat)

LILY. The decorator's coming tomorrow at ten, you have to clear out.

*(**LILY** won't look at her – she could crumble, but she won't.)*

*(**BLANCHE** releases her. **LILY** quickly makes her way to the door.)*

BLANCHE. *(desperate plea)* Look back!

*(**LILY** freezes.)*

Look: BACK.

(beat)

(a whisper) Mira hacia atrás, no me conviertas en piedra.

*(A long pause. **LILY** hesitates, then leaves.)*

Coward.

(beat)

I DON'T NEED YOU.

(silence)

(to herself, deeply unconvinced, she's sinking) I'll come out on top. I always knew I was meant for greatness. Deep inside A little voice I knew...I knew...

(She looks around at the cage she's built.)

(quiet) Help me.

(She smiles a sad smile.)

(plainly) I made bad choices... *(fighting tears) I made bad choices.*

3.

(A split scene:)

(On one part of the stage:
IKE *and* **LILY**.
That same evening.
Their bedroom.
He is finishing his pushups; **LILY** *is combing her hair.)*

(On another:
BLANCHE/IRIS *is alone in her basement room, packing her things, but very laxly. As she packs she composes a letter in her mind to "Bell."*
Bits of white paint still caked on her face.)

(She puts on a CD, a piece of Sibelius's, which plays softly in the background; a beautiful, lush, sad piece of music.)

(The realities overlap and merge here – there are no more discrete spaces, levels, it's all collapsed.)

*(***LILY*** brushes her hair, counting the strokes, beginning at 42, under her breath.*
IKE *is doing pushups, counting, beginning at 70.)*

LILY. Sixty-four, sixty-five, sixty-six

IKE. Ninety-two, ninety-three //

LILY. sixty-seven //

IKE. Sixty-eight, sixty-nine //

BLANCHE. The food at Gagnaire was perfect that night wasn't it bell? // He does wonders with radishes wouldn't you say? *wonders*

IKE. *Seventy.*

(He slumps to the floor exhausted. The music plays.)

LILY. seventy-one, seventy-two, seventy-three //

IKE. *(frustrated, down to* **BLANCHE***)* Fuckin *music* Turn that shit off!

LILY. seventy-four, seventy-five //

BLANCHE. I prefer him to Robuchon (although the pota-
toes at Robuchon oh my // *god*)

IKE. *(gingerly, very careful)* Whadja do today?

LILY. seventy-six, seventy-seven, seventy-eight, seventy-nine,
eighty, eighty-one //

IKE. Honey?

LILY. eighty-tw – *(Beat. Abstracted.)* What.

> *(The music continues to play.* **IKE** *looks at* **LILY**.*)*

IKE. Did you have a good day?

LILY. I went // to the

BLANCHE. *(rapt)* Oh // and *remember*

IKE. *(screams to basement/Blanche; fillip of rage)* SHUT-THE-
FUCK-UP.

> *(Nearly, but not quite simultaneously:*
> **BLANCHE** *jerks her head to the left, gasps, frightened –
> it's the ghost. The physical vocabulary here is identical
> to* **LILY***'s earlier in the play. She looks about the room,
> jarred.*
> **LILY** *jumps, drops her brush. Her face remains oddly
> expressionless.)*

(super sweet smile) Oh honey, did I scare you? I – I'm so
sorry

I didn't mean to do that...

I don't ever want to scare you.

> *(He picks up her brush, hands it to her.)*

Whatdyou say sweetheart?

(beat)

LILY. What? *(pause)* It's not important.

> *(***BLANCHE** *calms herself down, returns to the fantasy.)*

IKE. *(working to be attentive)* No no no – it's important. I
wanna know, I'm interested in what you do.

LILY. *(not responsive)* I had lunch.

BLANCHE. and the wines // (aha ha)

IKE. Who'd you go with.

LILY. No one. I went by myself.

(*She's staring in the mirror holding her brush.*)

IKE. You ok?

LILY. I like being by myself.

(**BLANCHE** *smiles – laughs quietly to herself for a moment.*)

IKE. You look nice //

(*He smiles.* **LILY** *doesn't.*)

BLANCHE. But that waiter He told me it was a Crozes Hermitage C-R-O and A HA HA and I must have looked // confused because

IKE. What'd you do somethin to ya hair I like it.

BLANCHE. because he…

(*She mumbles the rest to herself, giggles to herself quietly, packs.*)

(**LILY** *looks at* **IKE.**)

LILY. I don't want a live-in.

IKE. What.

(*beat*)

LILY. A girl. (*beat*) I can clean my own house.

IKE. We could get a day workah.

LILY. People steal.

(*beat*)

IKE. Whatever you want, it's…it's your decision, honey.

LILY. (*abstracted*) Thank you.

(*pause*)

IKE. You're letting em get to you.

LILY. No.

BLANCHE. (*bright*) I think Luce has a mind like a magnet. And we're like little iron filings she draws to her //

IKE. (*jarred*) People got short memories //

BLANCHE. We're // helpless

IKE. It'll all be in the past.

> (**LILY** *turns to him. She looks at him.*)

LILY. No. It *won't.*

BLANCHE. We're helpless but // that's

IKE. (*screaming, upset, no control*) YEAH-IT-WILL.

> (**BLANCHE** *gasps, jerks her head left; looks around the room, terrified.*)
>
> (*Recovering himself.* **IKE** *gets behind* **LILY**, *talking to her reflected image in the mirror.*)
>
> Anyways-screw-them-we-don-need-them-you-think-we-need-them?
>
> We don't need nothin from nobody.
>
> (*beat*)
>
> We got each other...Love is powerful...*Power* //

BLANCHE. (*a terrified whisper*) *What-are-you?*

> (**LILY** *jerks her head quickly to the side – she's seen something.*)
>
> (**BLANCHE** *jumps.*)
>
> [STOP]

LILY. I just saw it again.

> (*beat*)

IKE. Saw // what.

BLANCHE. *Who's there?*

> (*Beat. In the short silence* **BLANCHE**, *in a single gesture, pulls the gun from the suitcase. She holds her arms at her side. Stands very still, alert.*)

LILY. A face I saw it ...it was ...

> (**IKE** *starts laughing.*)
>
> (*She turns to him, looks at him – his cruelty is astonishing.*)

IKE. Ya didn't see anything.

(**LILY** *looks at him, not quite understanding.*)

LILY. (*somewhat dazedly*) I saw a face…

(**IKE** *walks over to her; her discombobulation makes him laugh harder.*)

IKE. (*though laughter*) Honey. I was playin a trick on you.

(**LILY** *just looks at him. She's sinking.* **IKE** *tries to stifle the laughter.*)

(**BLANCHE** *shudders.*)

BLANCHE. WHO'S-THERE?

(*points the gun*)

IKE. There's no ghost.

LILY. (*dying inside*) What?//

BLANCHE. (*terrified*) Get-outta-here! You-don't-exist!

(**IKE** *laughs – a private joke with himself.*)

(**BLANCHE** *pivots, points the gun.*)

IKE. (*laughter building*) I was having fun witchu!

(**LILY** *looks at* **IKE** *– practically looking through him. Her loneliness is palpable, she's faraway. The pain and humiliation she feels here builds though to the end of the scene.*)

Wha? don't look at me like that.

(**BLANCHE** *shudders, gasps audibly, as if someone's grabbed her from behind.*)

C'mere – //

BLANCHE. (*deep frustration, exhaustion*) I ain't scared a you! YOU-DON'T-EXIST!

(**IKE** *kisses* **LILY**'s *neck from behind. Music fades.*)

(*ferocious, desperate*) I-AIN'T-SCARED-A-YOU!

(**IKE** *slowly removes* **LILY**'s *clothes – she is very still, removed. Her eyes are frozen.*)

(**BLANCHE** *abruptly drops the bravado.*)

(She releases the gun weakly, it falls on the bed or to the ground. She covers her eyes with one hand, weeps helplessly. The lights begin to fade.)

BLANCHE. *(cont.)* *(to herself, weeping)* It don't end...

(We hear a car horn faintly in the distance.)

It don't end – I can't end it I can't...I can't
I can't...

(On the last "can't" we hear the car horn again, louder this time, two short beeps.)

I can't...

I can't...

I can't...

(We hear the car horn again, much louder, one long beep – it cuts off her last line as the lights go to black.)

(Once we hit total darkness there's a beat. Then:)

(Two loud beeps.)

(A pause.)

(One loud long beep.)

(Lights up on **LILY** *halfway down the stairs.)*

(It's the next morning, Bright.)

(As **LILY** *approaches the door to the basement we see* **BLANCHE** *lying on the floor in a corner, face down, gun not too far from her hand. Blood pooling around her head. She looks incidental to the surroundings, insignificant.)*

*(***LILY** *lingers in the stairwell, outside the door)*

LILY. *(through the door, tentative)* I heard something break, did you break something?

(pause)

Your car's outside

(pause)

LILY. *(cont.)* *(strained hauteur)* You better leave your address. So we can find you if we need you to – to pay for something. Th-th-there's expensive things in there.

(In the silence she starts to fall apart – she loses her comportment, any hauteur she was trying to project just falls away completely. Her emotion is all on the surface for this one instant and it's pulverizing; almost a whisper:)

Don't f-f-forget. Don't forget // to

(The car horn honks.)

(LILY *freezes back into her old rectilinear posture. Her face is a mask.)*

(no affect, faraway) Your car's outside.

(LILY *turns slowly. She walks to the foot of the staircase.)*

(She looks up, ascends. The car horn honks one last time.)

End of Play

OTHER TITLES AVAILABLE FROM SAMUEL FRENCH

KINDNESS

Adam Rapp

Drama / 2m, 2f / Interior

An ailing mother and her teenaged son flee Illinois and a crumbling marriage for the relative calm and safety of a midtown Manhattan hotel. Mom holds tickets to a popular musical about love among bohemians. Her son isn't interested, so Mom takes the kindly cabdriver instead, while the boy entertains a visitor from down the hall, an enigmatic, potentially dangerous young woman.

Kindness is a play about the possibility for sympathy in a harsh world and the meaning of mercy in the face of devastating circumstances.

Premiered at Playwrights Horizons, New York City in 2008.

"Compelling. A well-crafted mini-thriller, which keeps you in suspense until the final blackout."
– Joe Dziemianowics, *New York Daily News*

"Rapp has raised some provocative questions about the prickly mother/son relationship he has drawn in such detail."
– Marilyn Stasio, *Variety*

"Pungent, vivid...Rapp finds a gentle approach to his characters' physical and emotional pain without turning sentimental. His playful side is on display too." [Four stars]
– Diane Snyder, *Time Out New York*

"Adam Rapp can write dense, tense, funny dialogue."
– Charles Isherwood, *The New York Times*

"A taut and involving dark comedy. Hilarious and unsettling."
– Dan Bacalzo, *TheatreMania.com*